ASSESSMENT AND TREATMENT ACTIVITIES FOR CHILDREN, ADOLESCENTS AND FAMILIES: PRACTITIONERS SHARE THEIR MOST EFFECTIVE TECHNIQUES

Edited by
LIANA LOWENSTEIN

Champion Press
Toronto, Canada

National Library of Canada Cataloguing in Publication Data
Assessment and treatment activities for children, adolescents, and families: practitioners share their most effective techniques / edited by Liana Lowenstein.

ISBN 978-0-9685199-4-3

1. Child psychotherapy.   2. Family psychotherapy.   3. Play therapy.
4. Group psychotherapy for children.   5. Group psychotherapy for teenagers.
I. Lowenstein, Liana, 1965-

RC480.5.A87 2008   618.92'891653   C2008-905614-0

Correspondence regarding this book can be sent to:
Champion Press PO Box 91012, 2901 Bayview Avenue, Toronto, Ontario, Canada M2K 2Y6
Telephone: (416) 575-7836
Email: liana@globalserve.net
Web: www.lianalowenstein.com

About The Author

Liana Lowenstein, MSW, RSW, CPT-S, is a Registered Social Worker and Certified Play Therapist-Supervisor who has been working with children and their families since 1988. She provides clinical supervision and consultation to mental health practitioners and presents trainings across North America and abroad. She is the founder of Champion Press Publishing Company and has authored numerous publications, including the books *Paper Dolls and Paper Airplanes: Therapeutic Exercises for Sexually Traumatized Children* (with Crisci & Lay, 1997), *Creative Interventions for Troubled Children & Youth* (1999), *Creative Interventions for Bereaved Children* (2006), and *Cory Helps Kids Cope with Divorce* (2013). She has also edited the books *Assessment and Treatment Activities for Children, Adolescents, and Families: Practitioners Share Their Most Effective Techniques* (Volumes One through Three) and *Creative Family Therapy Techniques: Play, Art, and Expressive Activities to Engage Children in Family Sessions*. Ms. Lowenstein is winner of the Monica Hubert award for outstanding contribution and dedication to child psychotherapy and play therapy in Canada.

Also from Liana Lowenstein

Paper Dolls and Paper Airplanes:
Therapeutic Exercises for Sexually Traumatized Children
(Co-authored with Geraldine Crisci & Marilyn Lay)

Creative Interventions for Troubled Children and Youth

Creative Interventions for Bereaved Children

Creative Interventions for Children of Divorce

Assessment and Treatment Techniques for
Children, Adolescents, and Families:
Practitioners Share Their Most Effective Techniques
(Volumes One through Three)

Creative Family Therapy Techniques:
Play, Art, and Expressive Therapies to Engage Children in Family Sessions

Cory Helps Kids Cope with Divorce:
Playful Therapeutic Activities for Young Children

Cory Helps Kids Cope with Sexual Abuse:
Playful Activities for Traumatized Children

**For more information on the above books and
forthcoming publications, go to the author's website:
www.lianalowenstein.com**

Contributors

Katherine Arkell, MSW, LCSW
Vista Health, 2003-C S.E. Walton Blvd., Bentonville, AR 72712
Email: katherinea@vistahealthservices.com

Brenda Bierdeman, Psy.D., CPT-P
27 South Platt Street, Albion, NY 14411
Email: drbrenda@verizon.net

Kimberly Blackmore, MC
16 Woodcroft Place, Cambridge, ON N1P 1B1
Email: kimblack67@hotmail.com

Amy Brace, LMSW, ACSW
689 Abbey Mill Drive SE, Ada, MI 9301
Email: amykaybrace@yahoo.com

Donicka Budd, CYC (P-Cert)
Email: dbudd25@hotmail.com
Website: www.donickabudd.com

Felicia Carroll, M.Ed., MA
540 Alisal Rd. Ste. 1, Solvang, CA 93463
Email: Fcarroll@west.net
Webpage: www.feliciacarroll.com

Natalie Caufield, MSW, RSW
62 Frood Road, Sudbury, ON, P3C 4Z3
Email: caufield@bellnet.ca

Michelle Cotnoir, MSW, RSW
662 Falconbridge Rd, Sudbury, Ontario, P3A 4S4
Email: mcotnoir@childcare.on.ca

Mary Cowper-Smith, MSW, RSW
Families in Transition
700 Lawrence Ave. W., Ste. 420A, Box 129, Toronto, ON, M6A 3B4
Email: maryco@familyservicetoronto.org

David A. Crenshaw, Ph.D., ABPP, RPT-S
Rhinebeck Child & Family Center
Box 286, 23H East Market St., Rhinebeck, NY 12572
Website: www.rhinebeckcfc.com

Cynthia A. Dodge, Ph.D.
899 Riverside St, Portland, ME 04103
Email: cdodge@spurwink.org
Website: www.spurwink.org

Pam Dyson, MA, PLPC
15332 Manchester Road, Suite 209, Ellisville, MO 63011
Email: pam@pamdyson.com
Website: www.pamdyson.com

Kim L. Flournoy, MSW
2001 Rawlings St., Richmond, VA 23231
Email: flournoy.kim@gmail.com
Website: www.wirebird.upweb.com

Theresa Fraser, C.C.W., B.A
84 Acorn Way, Cambridge, ON, N1R 8M7
Email: theresafraser@rogers.com

Diane Frey, Ph.D., RPT-S
Wright State University
M072 Creative Arts Center, Dayton, OH 45435
Email: diane.frey@wright.edu

Deborah Armstrong Hickey, LMFT, RPT-S
4 Claret Drive, Greenville, South Carolina 29609
Email: Deborah.hickey@capella.edu

Susan T. Howson, MA, CPCC, CHBC
31 Ben Machree Drive, Port Credit, ON, L5H 2S2
Email: susan@magnificentcreations.com

Susan Kelsey, M.S., MFT, RPT-S
2900 Bristol Street, Suite G-101, Costa Mesa, CA 92626
Email: SusanKelseyMFT@cox.net

Sueann Kenney-Noziska, MSW, LISW, RPT-S
350 El Molino Boulevard, Las Cruces, NM 88005
Email: info@playtherapycorner.com
Website: www.playtherapycorner.com

Connie-Jean Latam, D.N.M.
1517 Brookview Drive, Kingsville, ON N9Y 2W6
Email: connie@cogeco.ca
Website: www.artoflivingresourcecentre.com

Norma Leben, MSW, LCSW, ACSW, RPT-S, CPT-P
Morning Glory Treatment Center for Children
1207 Pigeon Forge Rd, Pflugerville, TX 78660
Email: norma@playtherapygames.com
Website: www.playtherapygames.com

Christy L. Livingston, MFT
843 East Newton Lane, Placentia, CA 92870
Email: christy.livingston@yahoo.com

Sally A. Loughrin, LMSW, MA
Angela Hospice
14100 Newburgh Road, Livonia, Michigan 48154
Email: SALoughrin@aol.com

Liana Lowenstein, MSW, RSW, CPT-S
2901 Bayview Avenue, Box 91012, Toronto, ON, M2K 1H0
Email: liana@globalserve.net
Website: www.lianalowenstein.com

Tina Luna, BASc
14238 Dublin Line RR#3, Acton, ON, L7J 2L9
Email: tina.luna@gmail.com

Jennifer Mariaschin, LMSW
The Institute for Family Health River Center for Counseling
50-98 East 168th St, Bronx, New York 10452
Email: jmariaschin@institute2000.org

Kathryn A. Markell, Ph.D.

2478 Hamline Ave. N., Roseville, MN 55113

Email: ktmarkell@msn.com

Marc A. Markell, Ph.D., C.T

14081 Teal Court, Rogers, MN 55374

Email: mamarkell@stcloudstate.edu

Maxine McCleery Bowden, MA

855 N. Euclid Ave., Ontario, CA 91762

Email: mmccleerybowden@roadrunner.com

Sara McCool, MSW., LCSW., RPT

1400 E. Pugh Dr.,Ste. 10 (Kenbell Plaza), Terre Haute, IN 47802

Email: sara.e.mccool@gmail.com

Evangeline Munns, PhD.,CPsych., RPT-S

34 Burton Grove, King City, ON, L7B1C6

Email: emunns@sympatico.ca

Kim D. O'Connor, M.Ed.

458 Main Street, Kentville, NS B4N 1K8

Email: kimoconnor@ns.aliantzinc.ca

Website: www.kimoconnor.ca

Denise O'Neill, ECE C

936 Lorne Avenue, London, Ontario N5W 3L1

Email: jd_oneill@yahoo.ca

Website: www.patchforkids.ca

Sheila Ostroff, MA., CCC.CPT.CGRC.

2111 Northcliff, Suite# 351, N.D.G. Montreal, QC, H4A 3L6

Email: sheilaostroff@gmail.com

Leahanne Prolas, M.Ed
153 Lanigan Crescent, Stittsville, On K2S 1G9
Email: lprolas@yahoo.ca

Tammy Reis, MSW, RSW
Email: tammy_reis@yahoo.ca

Adriana Ribas, Ph.D.
Email: aribas@globo.com
Website: www.quartetoeditora.com.br

Maria Roberts, LCSW, RPT-S
12359 Sunrise Valley Drive, Suite 220, Reston, Virginia 20191
Email: mroberts@playtherapycenter.com

Cherilyn Rowland Petrie, L.M.H.C.
5487 North Ronald Reagan Boulevard, Sanford, FL 32773
Email: rowland@kidshouse.org

Lawrence Rubin, Ph.D., RPT-S
941 ne 19th Avenue, Suite 214, Fort Lauderdale, FL 33304
Email: lrubin@stu.edu

Ceilidh Eaton Russell, BA, CLSt. Dip.
Max and Beatrice Wolfe Centre for Children's Grief and Palliative Care
60 Murray Street, 4th Floor, Box 13, Toronto, Ontario M5T 3L9
Email: ceilidh.eatonrussell@tlcpc.org

Jodi Smith LCSW, RPT-S
201 W. 4th Street, Ste. 201, Claremont, CA 91711
Email: jodismith8997@verizon.net
Website: www.playispowerful.info

Chrissy Snead, M.Ed, LPC
2868 Acton Road, Birmingham, AL 35243
Email: chrissysnead@hotmail.com

Cyndi Starzyk-Frey, M.Ed., RSW

#408, 740 4th Ave. S. Lethbridge, AB. T1J 0N8

Email: cstarzyk@telus.net

Lisa Stein, MA

Promenade Mall, 1 Promenade Circle, Suite 301J, Thornhill, ON, L4J 4P8

Email: Lisa@lisasteintherapy.com

Jacqueline M. Swank, LCSW, RPT

Email: jacquelineswank@hotmail.com

Lysa Toye, MSW, RSW, Dip. EXAT

Max and Beatrice Wolfe Centre for Children's Grief and Palliative Care

60 Murray Street, 4th Floor, Box 13, Toronto ON M5T 3L9

Email: lysa.toye@tlcpc.org

Lorie Walton, M.Ed., CPT-S

Family First Play Therapy Centre Inc.

47 Holland St West, Box 1698, Bradford, ON L3Z 2B9

Email: familyfirstlw@bellnet.ca

Website: www.familyfirstplaytherapy.ca

Barbara Jones Warrick, M.Ed., CPT-S

941 Colborne St., London, ON N6A4A5

Email: bjw@vanier.com

Sarah Wells, BA

1064 Colborne Street, London, Ontario, N6A 4B3

Email: s.wells@merrymount.on.ca

Lynn R. Zakeri, LCSW

4254 Emerson St., Skokie, IL 60076

Email: lzakeri@gmail.com

Preface

When children are referred for therapy, they typically feel anxious and are reluctant to talk directly about their thoughts and feelings. Activities that are creative and play-based can engage children and help them to safely express themselves. The interventions presented in this book aim to capture and sustain children's interest and motivation in therapy, while helping them express themselves within the context of a safe therapeutic environment.

This publication provides a medium for practitioners to share their most effective assessment and treatment interventions. When I invited practitioners to contribute techniques to this publication, I was impressed with the range of creative ideas submitted.

The activities in this publication have been divided into the following sections: Engagement and Assessment, Feelings Expression, Social Skills, Coping & Problem-Solving, Self-Esteem, and Termination. The book begins with assessment activities providing clinicians with diagnostic tools to assist in treatment planning. The remaining sections provide activities to help clients master key emotional and behavioral competencies, such as identifying and expressing feeling states, strengthening interpersonal skills, learning coping strategies, and enhancing self-esteem. A variety of activities are provided within each section, so that practitioners can choose interventions that suit their clients' specific needs.

The last section of the book presents interventions that can be incorporated as part of the client's termination process.

Each activity is described within a framework that recommends age suitability and preferred treatment modality. Goals for the activity are outlined. Materials needed to complete the activity are listed. The book includes detailed instructions for all activities and a discussion section that further clarifies application and process.

Practitioners using the interventions in this publication should be well-trained in therapeutic intervention with children. A warm and caring rapport must be established with the client, and the activities should be implemented using sound clinical principles.

I hope this collection of interventions helps to create an engaging and meaningful therapeutic experience for your clients.

Liana Lowenstein

Acknowledgments

This is my first edited book and I am grateful for those who helped make the process a pleasurable and worthwhile experience. My heartfelt thanks are due first to the many talented practitioners who contributed to this book. Thanks to Beth McAuley for her editorial skills, and to Robyn Naster for proofreading the manuscript. Thanks to Kim Bracic and Dave Friesen at Hignell Book Printing for their help in bringing this book to print. I also thank Jacques Lauzon for his hi-tech computer assistance.

Special thanks to my family, friends, and colleagues for their ongoing support and encouragement. I give my greatest thanks to Steven, who is a wonderful husband and father, and to Jaime, whose love and laughter I treasure.

Contents

Section One: Engagement and Assessment

Section Two: Feelings Expression

Section Three: Social Skills

Section Four: Coping and Problem-Solving

Section One:
Engagement and Assessment

The "Talking Ball" Game
Source: Norma Leben

Theme: Engagement and Assessment
Recommended Age Range: Five to Adult
Treatment Modality: Group, Family

Goals
- Promote interaction and communication among members of the group or family
- Empower the quiet or timid members to initiate conversation and receive information they need
- Build trust among players

Materials
- A ball

Description
The practitioner tells the group or family that they are going to play the "Talking Ball" Game and explains the rules as follows:

"The ball is rolled from one member to another member across the table. That receiver will answer the question asked by the sender. The receiver then rolls the ball to another member and asks that member a question. That member answers the question. The game continues in this manner for five to ten minutes or until every player has a chance to ask three questions. The questions must be geared to getting to know each other."

The practitioner starts the game by rolling the ball to the quietest member and asks a simple question such as, "What is your favorite food?" That person should answer the question and then they ask another player a question by rolling a ball towards that person.

Discussion
This game can be played at different stages of group development. In the pre-affiliative stage, this is an engaging way for members to get acquainted with one another's likes, dislikes, interests, hobbies, favorite subjects, birth place, and so on.

At a later stage of group development, this game can be used as an intervention technique in several different ways:

Making a direct compliment: "I like how you are kind to everyone."
Sharing a feeling: "Lately, I'm annoyed and concerned about you not having

2

dinner with us."

Processing group dynamics and relationship issues: "I'm aware that you've been avoiding eye contact with me. Have I offended you in any way?"

The practitioner may need to help the younger members formulate their questions in order to get the information they want. In families, children may use this "ball power" to ask their siblings and parents difficult questions about unfair treatment, favoritism towards another family member, sicknesses, drunken habits, unsafe driving, physical violence, pending divorce, job changes, moving away, and other hard-to-bring-up topics.

Based on the questions asked, the practitioner can assess members' worries and concerns. A player's answers can also reveal much about that person's openness, honesty, loyalty, values, beliefs, and general personality. The practitioner may coach the group about trust and openness using this game to demonstrate that those who are willing to disclose personal information are more invested in the group and may earn more trust from others. Trust is the key component to healthy relationships and group cohesiveness.

About The Author
Norma Leben, MSW, LCSW, ACSW, RPT-S, CPT-P. Since graduating with a University of Chicago MSSA, Norma has worked as a CPS supervisor, school dropout team leader, residential treatment supervisor, executive director, and international trainer. She is a licensed clinical social worker and play therapy supervisor who has authored over 45 audio or video recordings, books, and publications in English and Chinese on parenting and play therapy techniques.

Brain Work
Source: Kim L. Flournoy

Theme: Engagement and Assessment
Recommended Age Range: Six to Ten
Treatment Modality: Individual

Goals
- Clarify the purpose, roles, and process of therapy
- Establish a safe and open therapeutic environment
- Gather information about the client

Materials
- Dry erase board and markers, eraser (or paper and erasable pencils)

Description
The practitioner begins the activity by stating, "Lots of times children are confused about why they come here ... some feel scared because they don't know what's going to happen." The practitioner moves to the dry erase board and introduces Brain Work.

The practitioner draws two simple faces without mouths and leaves the top third of the circle blank. The practitioner explains that one face depicts the child and the other depicts the practitioner.

In the top third of each face, the practitioner draws a large brain using squiggly lines in an oblong shape. The practitioner asks, "What kinds of things happen in brains?" and prompts, "Thinking happens in brains." The practitioner continues, "What fills up your brain? What takes up a lot of space in your brain that you wish wasn't there? Or what does your brain worry about a lot?" The practitioner may have to assist the child in identifying this issue (typically the child's reason for referral).

The practitioner draws a simple picture of the child's identified issue as filling in the entire empty brain. The practitioner and child discuss "all of the fun stuff" that could be in her/his brain "if only there was space!" The practitioner then explains that making space in the child's brain is the purpose of therapy: "To get that stuff out and make room for stuff you want to be in there!" This is his/her Brain Work.

The practitioner reminds the child of the absence of mouths in the pictures and asks the child to draw the expression (mouth) that goes with the identified issue (typically sad or mad). The practitioner then draws a relatively neutral expression on his/her face (such as a straight line) and explains that the child's feelings are the

4

most important feelings in therapy.

The practitioner draws a line with an arrow from the child's full brain to the practitioner's empty brain while asking the child, "So, how do we get that yucky stuff out of your brain and into mine?" The practitioner then explains to the child the particular therapeutic methods (art, play, talk, etc.) he/she uses.

Finally, as the practitioner draws the child's presenting issue into his/her empty brain, the practitioner directs the child to "erase the yucky stuff" from the child's brain. The practitioner then prompts the child to alter her/his facial expression to reflect the absence of the "yucky stuff" in the brain. The practitioner explains, "What you put in my brain stays in my brain … my job is to hold that for you."

Discussion

Many children come to therapy confused, fearful, or unsure of the therapeutic process. This intervention provides children with a step-by-step and visual way to age-appropriately understand complicated concepts, such as the purpose of therapy, their role and the practitioner's role in therapy, and confidentiality. The intervention also provides children with a visual representation of the practitioner as a safe container for their feelings.

Brain Work can be used throughout therapy as a way to monitor progress ("The yucky stuff doesn't take up as much space in my brain as last session"). Progress on a dry erase board can be documented with digital pictures. Brain Work also explains the concept of termination such as "When there's no more yucky stuff filling your brain …"

About the Author

Kim L. Flournoy, MSW, is the Director of Children's Services for Safe Harbor, a comprehensive domestic violence program. She was the first recipient of the Virginia Sexual and Domestic Violence Action Alliance's Blue Ribbon Award for excellence in children's advocacy. She developed and taught an international distance-learning course on play therapy. She serves on numerous boards and committees related to trauma and children. As a freelance consultant, she provides training on child trauma, play therapy, and vicarious trauma.

Call-Outs: Learning the Language
Source: Jodi Smith

Theme: Engagement and Assessment
Recommended Age Range: Twelve to Sixteen
Treatment Modality: Individual, Group

Goals
- Establish a positive and open therapeutic environment
- Increase open communication
- Gather information about the client

Materials
- Cardstock or construction paper
- Markers
- Call-out template (included)

Advance Preparation
Cut out call-outs (use template provided) using different colored paper.

Description
Explain the activity as follows:

"On each call-out write a word, term, or saying that you and your friends use. Make sure to include at least one saying your parent/guardian hates, one saying you would never say in front of a parent and/or teacher, and one saying you don't think I will know. On the back of each call-out, write the meaning of the saying."

Once done, the clients can share their call-out cards, their meanings, how they use them, and which of the above categories they fit into.

Discussion
Teenagers often speak their own language. Some use words that they pick up on TV, some use words universal to teenagers, some have words that are created/used just within their own group, some are geographical and some are generational. These words help teenagers express themselves in a unique way that separates them from the adult word. Sometimes these words are used to mislead adults or conceal the true meaning of what is being said.

Learning the language of teens demonstrates genuine interest and acceptance of them. This facilitates positive rapport and open communication.

A variation of this activity is to make it into a game in which the clients challenge the practitioner to guess the meaning of each call-out.

About The Author
Jodi Smith, MSW, LCSW, RPT-S, is a Licensed Clinical Social Worker and Registered Play Therapist Supervisor specializing in using play therapy in clinical practice with children, adolescents and their families, as well as with adults. Jodi is currently the Director of Norton-Fisher Child & Family Programs for West End Family Counseling. Additionally, she maintains a private practice in Claremont, California, and is a part-time lecturer for the USC School of Social Work.

Call-Outs: Template

Play-Doh-Nary
Source: Christy L. Livingston

Theme: Engagement and Assessment
Recommended Age Range: Six to Sixteen
Treatment Modality: Individual, Group, Family

Goals
- Establish a positive and open therapeutic environment
- Evaluate fine motor skills
- Discuss feelings of frustration and identify ways to handle frustration

Materials
- Play-Doh
- Item Cards (included)
- Timer
- Pen or pencil
- Paper
  (Alternatively, you may use the cranium game Sculptorades™ for similar materials.)

Description
Decide who goes first by asking the client to choose or by finding the person whose birthday is up next. Shuffle the Item Cards and place them in a pile, face down (or order the cards so that easier items to sculpt are at the top of the pile).

The first person picks up a card and reads it, without revealing the item to the other players. Turn over the timer and begin to sculpt the item on the card, using the Play-Doh.

The first person to guess the item correctly wins the point. If no one guesses correctly by the end of the timer, no one gets the point. The winner is decided by tallying who collected the most points at the end of the game.

At the end, process the activity by asking questions such as, "What was the most frustrating part of this game?" "Tell me about other times when you have felt frustrated recently?" "What are some ways to handle frustration?"

Discussion
The Item Cards include feeling words and items to prompt discussion. Many of the items are in the play therapy room and therefore may help the client become more familiar with play therapy resources. Also included are six blank subject cards for the practitioner to add extra items, if desired. The Item Cards can be adapted, depending

9

on the age and needs of the client.

The practitioner facilitates a discussion of frustration during the processing phase. It may be beneficial to discuss what led to any feelings of frustration and how these feelings affected their ability to communicate with one another.

This game may be modified depending on the treatment modality. In group or family sessions, clients may choose to form teams. This will help increase cohesion and social skills building.

About The Author
Christy L. Livingston, MFT, is a post-graduate resident at West End Family Counseling Services in Rancho Cucamonga, California. She is completing her internship hours at Heritage Intermediate School in the Etiwanda School District. She presented research at the American Psychological Society Conference (2005) on learning and memory with aging populations.

© Christy L. Livingston

Play-Doh-Nary
Item Cards

STAR	HAPPY	MAD
GUN	HEART	HAND
HOUSE	CROWN	MOUTH

LEGO	TURTLE	CASTLE
SAD	CELL PHONE	PEN
EYE	BABY BOTTLE	MAGIC WAND

Therapeutic Magic Tricks
Source: Diane Frey

Theme: Engagement and Assessment
Recommended Age Range: Five and Up
Treatment Modality: Individual, Group

Goals
- Establish a non-threatening therapeutic environment
- Provide insight about behavior change
- Encourage hopefulness in the client(s)
- Encourage creative problem-solving

Materials
- Rubber band
- Potato
- Straw
- Drinking glass
- Water

Description
Each of these three magic tricks helps the client to develop new insights into the possibilities of change. The tricks also provide the client with insights about creative problem-solving.

In the Jumping Rubber Band magic trick, the practitioner tells the client that she/he can make a rubber band jump from her/his small and ring finger to the fore and middle finger. The practitioner puts the rubber band over her/his small and ring finger, then folds all four finger tips under the inside of the rubber band, folding the fingers towards the palm of the hand. The rubber band automatically jumps from the two fingers it was on to the fore and middle finger.

In the Drink the Water magic trick, the practitioner places a glass of water on an outstretched right hand, and asks the client to grip her/his right arm with both hands. The practitioner says that, despite her/his effort to hold down the client's arm, she/he can lift the glass to her/his mouth and drink the water. As soon as the client has tightened his/her grip, the practitioner reaches out with the left hand, lifts the glass from the right palm up to her/his mouth, and drinks the water.

In the Straw and the Potato magic trick, the client is given a straw and a potato and is challenged to push the straw into the potato. The client will attempt this but will not succeed. The practitioner then tries. The practitioner folds over one end of the straw, grips it in his/her hand, takes the other end of the straw and pushes it into the potato. The reason for the change is that air is compressed in the straw when the end of the straw is folded, therefore, the straw will penetrate the potato.

Discussion

Numerous clients present resistance to counseling for various reasons. Since most people have a positive association and curiosity about magic, the technique is often very helpful in minimizing resistance, engaging the client, and establishing rapport. Even the most negative client will usually watch the practitioner do a magic trick. The three tricks described here all have a theme of helping the client to understand that although she/he might think change is impossible for her/him, with additional knowledge it is possible. Although the client may feel entrenched in a behavior pattern, the practitioner can help her/him to develop creative problem-solving.

In addition to these uses, other magic can be used in therapy to encourage self-expression, teach life skills, provide reinforcement for appropriate behavior, serve as a diagnostic aid, enhance self-esteem, and infuse therapy with pleasure.

In using magic in therapy, certain guidelines need to be observed. Practitioners need to use magic that is age appropriate for the client. As contrasted to stage magic, magic in therapy involves teaching the client how to do the trick, thus empowering the client.

It is important to use magic that facilitates interaction between the practitioner and the client. Magic used in therapy should have embedded therapeutic metaphors such as the ones discussed with the aforementioned examples. Always avoid magic that has "trickiness" associated with it (i.e., false bottoms of containers, fake cards). Seek genuine straightforward magic tricks that the client can easily learn. Always use tricks that are safe for the client (i.e., no use of matches, materials that could be harmful). Use tricks that can be done with materials easily accessible to children and/or older clients. Avoid using magic with clients who have poor reality testing or psychosis.

It is still true today what Carl Jung said many years ago, "The hands know how to solve a riddle with which the intellect struggles in vein." Assisting clients to use their hands in magic is a highly facilitative process.

Reference
Frey, D. (2001). *Using magic in play therapy.* Dayton, Ohio: Mandala Publishing.

About the Author
Diane Frey, Ph.D., R.P.T.S, is a professor at Wright State University in Dayton, Ohio, where she also is in private practice as a licensed clinical psychologist. Dr. Frey has authored 17 books and numerous chapters in texts and curriculum materials. She is an internationally recognized speaker on such topics as play therapy, self-esteem, the psychosocial emotional needs of the gifted, and emotional intelligence.

Scavenger Hunt
Source: Liana Lowenstein

Theme: Engagement and Assessment
Recommended Age Range: Seven and Up
Treatment Modality: Group

Goals
- Increase group cohesion
- Assess and improve the group members' problem-solving abilities
- Increase open communication

Materials
- List of scavenger hunt items
- Score sheet

Advance Preparation
Develop a list of scavenger hunt items for the group members to collect. The list can be modified, depending on the age of the clients and the issues to be addressed in the session. For example, scavenger hunt items for a group of children dealing with divorce can include: (1) a written definition of divorce, (2) an outline of a hand, (3) five feelings children may have when parents divorce, (4) two people with the same shoe size, (5) words of advice to help children who feel the divorce was their fault, (6) a group of children holding hands and singing a song.

Description
Explain the activity as follows:

"You will be divided into two teams. Each team will get a list of scavenger hunt items. You will have 15 minutes to collect as many items on the list that you can. Some of the items will need to be gathered from around the room, and some of the items will need to be created. Some of the items will require creativity. You will be awarded one point for each item you collect. You will be awarded extra points for teamwork, creativity, and positive behavior."

A group leader should be assigned to each group to assist with reading and writing and to facilitate appropriate group interaction.

Discussion
This intervention promotes communication regarding divorce, catharsis of feelings, and problem-solving. It encourages creative thinking and open dialogue among group members.

Reference

Lowenstein, L. (2006). *Creative interventions for children of divorce.* Toronto, ON: Champion Press.

About The Author

Liana Lowenstein, MSW, RSW, CPT-S, is a social worker and Certified Play Therapy Supervisor in Toronto. She maintains a private practice, provides clinical supervision and consultation to mental health professionals, and lectures internationally on child and play therapy. She has authored numerous publications, including the books *Paper Dolls and Paper Airplanes: Therapeutic Exercises for Sexually Traumatized Children, Creative Interventions for Troubled Children and Youth, More Creative Interventions for Troubled Children and Youth, Creative Interventions for Bereaved Children,* and *Creative Interventions for Children of Divorce.*

Mirroring Activity
Source: Evangeline Munns

Theme: Engagement and Assessment
Recommended Age Range: Three and Up
Treatment Modality: Individual, Family

Goals:
- Increase attunement between two or more individuals
- Improve self-control
- Improve ability to follow directions from someone else

Description
Explain the activity as follows:

"I want you to stand in front of me just right there (pointing to a spot about two feet in front of the practitioner). You are going to be my mirror. Everything I do you will try to copy, but the trick is to copy me at exactly the same time that I am doing it, so you are my mirror. I will go slowly so you have a chance to think about where I will be moving so we can do it exactly at the same time. We can't touch each other. I will lead first and then you will take a turn leading. Ready? Here we go!"

Discussion
This activity is an amazingly effective one for bringing two or more individuals (if working with a family) into attunement with each other. The participants have to be fully attentive, engaged, and sensitive to each other. It also motivates the individuals to be co-operative with each other. The practitioner needs to correct the movements of the leading person if she/he is going too fast, because then the follower will only be able to imitate (be a few seconds later in copying the movements) rather than truly mirror what the leader is doing.

If the leader starts to move into difficult positions with her/his hands or body, then the practitioner may suggest, "Just keep it simple," so the follower has an easier time to truly mirror the action. The practitioner may suggest that the leader just move the hands at first.

This is an effective activity for increasing the attunement between parent and child, between siblings or peers, and has also been used in marital therapy.

About The Author
Evangeline Munns, PhD., CPsych., RPT-S, is a registered clinical psychologist in King City, north of Toronto, Ontario. She has her own psychological consultant

services and is a certified supervisor and trainer with the Canadian Association for Child and Play Therapy (CACPT), the American Association for Play Therapy (APT), and the Theraplay® Insititute in Chicago. She is a popular presenter nationally and internationally. Dr. Munns has authored many articles and her book *Theraplay: Innovations in Attachment Enhancing Play Therapy,* will be followed in the near future with her second book, *Applications of Family and Group Theraplay.*

© Evangeline Munns

It's My Life CD
Source: Jodi Smith

Theme: Engagement and Assessment
Recommended Age Range: Twelve and Up
Treatment Modality: Individual

Goals
- Establish a non-threatening therapeutic environment
- Gather information about client's life and perceptions of her/his past

Materials
- Empty plastic CD jewel case
- Paper, construction paper, markers, colored pencils

Advance Preparation
Cut several pieces of paper to fit inside the jewel case.

Description
Begin by exploring the client's musical taste and favorite musicians, bands, and CDs. Present the client with the empty jewel case and explain that she/he will be designing her/his own CD. This will include:

- the CD title
- a cover design
- a playlist

The CD theme can be as vague as "This CD will be about your life," or more specific, such as focusing on a specific treatment issue (i.e., anger, grief, and so on).

Clients can create fictitious song titles for their playlist or select real songs that have meaning for them, or a combination of the two.

Discussion
Many teenagers are immersed in the world of music. Music lyrics often elicit strong emotions, normalizing and expressing their emotions in ways that they either cannot or do not feel safe doing. This connection to music is a great way to begin to establish a relationship with teen clients in a non-threatening manner.

The information gathered from this project can be used as a springboard for further discussions and activities. Some clients can then create lyrics to some of the songs on their playlist. The practitioner may also suggest additional CDs to work on, such as "Greatest Hits" (focusing on self-esteem) or "Volume II: My Future" (focusing on goals). The possibilities are endless.

About The Author

Jodi Smith, MSW, LCSW, RPT-S, is a Licensed Clinical Social Worker and Registered Play Therapist Supervisor specializing in using play therapy in clinical practice with children, adolescents and their families, as well as with adults. Jodi is currently the Director of Norton-Fisher Child & Family Programs for West End Family Counseling. Additionally, she maintains a private practice in Claremont, California, and is a part-time lecturer for the USC School of Social Work.

The Magic Key
Source: David A. Crenshaw

Theme: Engagement and Assessment
Recommended Age Range: Nine to Fourteen
Treatment Modality: Individual, Group

Goals
- Verbally identify key issues to address in therapy
- Increase awareness of losses, particularly unacknowledged or disenfranchised grief
- Verbally express denied or disconnected feelings about prior losses
- Expand therapeutic dialogue about the issues that matter most to the child

Materials
- Paper
- Markers
- Pencil or Colored Pencils
- Crayons

Description
Read the following instructions to the child:

"Imagine that you have been given a magic key that opens one room in a huge castle. There are four floors in the castle and since the castle is huge there are many rooms on each floor, but your magic key only opens one of the many, many rooms in the castle. Pretend you go from room to room, and from floor to floor, trying your magic key in each door until you finally come to the door that your key opens. You turn the key and the lock opens. Because you have been given a magic key that only opens this door, what you see is the one thing that money can't buy that you always thought would make you happy. Pretend that you are looking into the room. What is it that you see? What is that one thing that has been missing that you think would make you happy? When you have a clear picture, please draw it as best you can."

Discussion
Projective drawing and storytelling strategies along with therapeutic play and the use of symbols are central to tools used in therapy with children and adolescents (Crenshaw, 2004; 2006; 2008). "The Magic Key" (Crenshaw, 2004; Crenshaw & Mordock, 2005; Crenshaw, 2008) is a projective drawing strategy that was developed to evoke themes of loss, longing, and missing in the lives of children.

In early versions of this strategy, the caveat "that money can't buy" was not included in the directions. It is not surprising in this highly consumer-oriented culture that many children drew a big-screen television or the latest video game console. Some children, however, drew a missing or deceased parent, a safe home they never experienced, or a family where the parents didn't argue. They drew a home they always longed for, one that sadly was missing in their lives. By adding the qualifier "that money can't buy," the strategy focuses the child on the essential emotional needs that have not been met or on the important losses that the child has suffered rather than on the latest electronic gadget or toy.

This projective drawing strategy is especially useful with children whose lives are replete with loss. Many severely aggressive children have suffered profound, multiple losses (Crenshaw & Garbarino, 2007; Crenshaw & Hardy, 2005; Crenshaw & Mordock, 2005). This strategy is one of the ways to access these feelings when children are disconnected from their emotions or have great difficulty verbalizing their painful affect. Issues of timing and pacing, including the readiness of the child to undertake emotionally focused work, are critical. Before using this tool readers should review "The Play Therapy Decision Grid" (Crenshaw & Mordock, 2005) and determine whether the child is appropriate for the Coping or Invitational Track of therapy. This technique should only be used with children who are judged to be ready for the Invitational Track. Children appropriately assigned to the Invitational Track will be judged as having adequate ego strengths, mature defenses, ability to manage anxiety, and the ability to tolerate and contain strong emotion without becoming overwhelmed. The child in the Invitational Track will not show signs of "spillover" from therapy sessions resulting in disruptive anxiety and behavior during or immediately following the session. The name of the Invitational Track is meant to imply that the child is invited to go as far as she/he can at any one point in time in approaching the painful affect or events that need to be faced and resolved.

Tools, such as "The Magic Key," are meant to expand and enrich the therapeutic dialogue and do not constitute therapy itself. The therapy process entails much more than the application of tools such as this, but they can facilitate meaningful dialogue, which can aid the healing process. Whatever drawing the child produces in response to the directions to "The Magic Key" will serve as a springboard to elicit more of the child's feelings, wishes, fears, dreams, hopes, and will create a portal of entry into the child's inner life.

References
Crenshaw, D.A. (2004). *Engaging resistant children in therapy: Projective drawing and storytelling strategies*. Rhinebeck, NY: Rhinebeck Child and Family Center Publications.

Crenshaw, D.A. (2006). *Evocative strategies in child and adolescent psychotherapy*. New York: Jason Aronson.

Crenshaw, D.A. (2008). *Therapeutic engagement of children and adolescents: Play, symbol, drawing, and storytelling strategies*. New York: Jason Aronson.

Crenshaw, D.A. & J.B. Mordock. (2005). *Handbook of play therapy with aggressive children.* New York: Jason Aronson.

Crenshaw, D.A. & J. Garbarino. (2007). "The hidden dimensions: Profound sorrow and buried human potential in violent youth." *Journal of Humanistic Psychology,* 47, 160-174.

Crenshaw, D.A. & K.V. Hardy. (2005). "Understanding and treating the aggression of traumatized children in out-of-home care." *In N. Boyd-Webb, ed., Working with traumatized youth in child welfare, pp. 171–195.* New York: Guilford.

About The Author

David A. Crenshaw, Ph.D., ABPP, is a Board Certified Clinical Psychologist by the American Board of Professional Psychology and a Registered Play Therapist Supervisor by the Association for Play Therapy. He is the author of *Therapeutic Engagement of Children and Adolescents: Play, Symbol, Drawing and Storytelling Strategies; Evocative Strategies in Child and Adolescent Psychotherapy;* and co-author with John B. Mordock of the *Handbook of Play Therapy with Aggressive Children and Understanding the Aggression of Children: Fawns in Gorilla Suits.* He is the editor of a new book, *Child and Adolescent Psychotherapy: Wounded Spirits and Healing Paths.*

Lifeline

Source: Felicia Carroll and Adriana Ribas

Theme: Engagement and Assessment
Recommended Age Range: Seven and Up
Treatment Modality: Individual

Goals
- Learn more about the child's life from the child's perspective
- Increase a child's ability to organize her/his sense of self
- Develop a child's ability to express feelings about her/his self, life events, and significant people
- Develop the child's awareness of her/his choices in creating the future

Materials
- Large piece of paper
- Markers
- Scissors
- Glue
- Magazines
- Scrap items that can be used for art

Description
The practitioner invites the child to take part in an activity about her/his life. The activity involves outlining the child's life onto a piece of paper.

The first step is to give the child a large piece of paper and ask her/him to draw a horizontal line across the middle of the paper. At one end of the line, the practitioner writes down the child's date of birth. At the other end, place the projected year which the child imagines would represent the length of her/his life. For instance, a child's birth date might be 1998, making her/him 10 years old at the time of creating the lifeline and she/he might imagine living to be 85 years old. So, the year at the other end of her/his life would be 2083. The practitioner then divides the line into four segments and then into eight segments and then into sixteen segments. Each segment represents approximately five years of the child's life. The practitioner then draws a second line the same length as the lifeline that represents the age of the child. So it begins with the birth date and ends with age 10. This allows more space for the details of the child's life.

The child then illustrates significant life events on the lifeline by writing words, drawing pictures, creating a collage, pasting on personal photographs, and so on. The practitioner can facilitate this process by asking questions about important events, milestones, and significant people in the child's life. As the child begins to slowly recall the easy events such as birthdays, preschool, or births of siblings, other more difficult events will be remembered.

The practitioner processes this activity by asking questions about events, feelings experienced, and significant people identified in the lifeline. The practitioner encourages the child to recall as much detail as the child is comfortable sharing. It is important to explore the child's perceptions and feelings about the past and integrate them into the present. For instance, "How did you feel when this happened? How do you feel now? Is there any difference?" Another helpful question to ask is, "If you had a way of changing anything that has occurred in the past to make your life better today, what would you do?"

Another facet of this activity is to look at how much of the lifeline remains. If the child is 10, for example, and the lifeline is projected at 85 years, then 75 years lie ahead. These years can be filled in with the child's fantasies, expectations and hopes — for example, going to college, writing a first novel by 30, learning to drive a car, travelling the world, getting married, taking early retirement. If the child is having difficulty envisioning her/his future, the practitioner can ask prompt questions such as, "What do you hope to be when you grow up and what kind of schooling would you need in order to do that? Do you see yourself remaining single, or getting married? Would you like to have children? Where in the world would you like to visit? When you are not working, what do you think you will want to do for fun? What one thing do you want to have in your future that money cannot buy? What do you hope will be your biggest life achievement?"

Discussion

This activity helps a child understand that her/his life is unique and that every child has a different life story. It allows a child to reflect on the processes of change and growth. It can also stimulate children to begin creating a cohesive narrative that can provide her/him with support in coping with past trauma as well as present challenges and accomplishments. Furthermore, through thinking about the events of her/his life while in contact with another person, she/he can be supported in actively imagining the possibilities for the future.

This technique was inspired by the works of Bruner (1965) and Hobday and Ollier (1998).

References

Bruner, J. S. (1965). "Man: A Course of Study." Occasional Paper No. 3. in *Education Development Center, The Social Studies Curriculum Program.* Cambridge: Social Educational Services.

Hobday, A., & K. Ollier. (1998). *Creative therapy with children and adolescents.* Atascadero: Impact Publishers.

About The Authors

Felicia Carroll, MEd, MA, is a licensed Marriage and Family Therapist and Registered Play Therapist-Supervisor in private practice. She is the Director of the West Coast Institute of Gestalt Play Therapy in Solvang, California. She conducts training programs for mental health professionals internationally and has written chapters in books about Gestalt Therapy with children and adolescents. Felicia was a classroom teacher for twelve years before becoming a therapist.

Adriana Ribas is a Licensed Psychologist in the Regional Council of Psychology, Brazil. She is full professor at the Estacio de Sa University in Rio de Janeiro, where she earned her Ph.D. in psychology. She works as a clinical psychologist and has written numerous publications about parenting, adult-child interaction, and infant development.

Assessing Parent Empathy Through Sandtray
Source: Deborah Armstrong Hickey

Theme: Engagement and Assessment
Recommended Age Range: Parent/Caregiver Adult
Modality: Family (Parents/Caregivers)

Goals
- Increase and deepen parents/caregivers self-awareness
- Increase and deepen parents/caregivers understanding of their child and what may be influencing the behavioral symptoms
- Increase and deepen empathic regard for the child
- Allow for a more balanced view of the problem and open up space for creative problem-solving

Materials
- Two sandtrays: one large and one small (optional)
- Sandtray symbols (or objects of nature)

Description
This assessment intervention involves three processes. All of these processes involve the use of sandtrays and sandtray symbols. A large collection of symbols is not necessary. In fact, objects of nature can be used and it would be possible to do this exercise without using the sandtrays.

The practitioner explains that she/he wants to get to know something about how the parents see themselves as being ideal parents/caregivers of their child, who they aspire to be, or even who they may be occasionally.

The practitioner explains that he/she also wants to help them connect to what it is that may lie beneath the behaviors that their child is exhibiting, to understand who their child is and what they may be needing to do to help the child, and to find ways to reduce these symptoms.

The practitioner asks each parent to first choose a symbol that represents them as the "optimal" parent ... the one who cares and understands deeply and parents wisely. The practitioner gives the parents ample time to choose and to place their symbols on the small sandtray. The practitioner invites the parents to notice feelings, thoughts, and images that surface as they see the symbols before them. Nothing needs to be shared at this point.

Next, the practitioner asks the parents to choose a symbol that expresses their child behaving "badly" … this can be said with discernment and humor, depending on the circumstances and symptoms. This symbol is to express their child's outward behaviors, what they are expressing in the world. The parents are asked to place their symbols on the large sandtray.

The practitioner then asks the parents to just sit and take in the symbols that express their child's symptoms and, when ready, to choose a symbol that expresses their child's interior experience that may be driving these symptoms. The practitioner suggests that the parents choose this symbol not from the head but from the heart and to "let their fingers do the walking" (Speert, 2000). The parents are asked to place this symbol on the large sandtray with the other symbol that represents the child's symptoms and behaviors.

The two sandtrays, both small and large, are placed where everyone can see them.

Following these steps, a discussion can begin about what the parents learned from the processes, anything that was surprising or of value, and anything that informed them about what the child may be needing from them or feeling. In particular, the practitioner can begin a dialogue about what the "optimal" parents/caregivers might change in their relationship with their child, knowing what they know now.

If the process seems stuck or the parents seem uncertain, the practitioner can do, say, or move in any number of directions, including inviting the parents to choose an object with their heart, not their head, that may represent what the child or they need to change in order to achieve want they want to change; asking the parents to hold the symbol that represents the child's interior, close their eyes, and imagine what the child might want them to know about what they are feeling and needing; or simply request that the parents let what has been experienced percolate for a week and see what they come back with in the following session.

The practitioner can begin the next session by using the sandtrays as they have been left and pick up the dialogue as a way to revisit this process.

The intervention used in this manner fits most appropriately into the assessment phase of treatment. In future sessions, any of these symbols can be revisited for review and discussions about progress or changes.

Discussion

This assessment activity is helpful to use with parents/caregivers who are experiencing difficulty with their child. The assessment process usually involves a minimum of two sessions with the parents/caregivers, followed by two to three sessions with the child or adolescent, followed by a session with the parents/caregivers to make treatment recommendations.

Parents/caregivers who engage in this exercise find it meaningful in several important ways. First, it usually allows them to feel hope when they imagine themselves as the parents/caregivers they want to be. They feel reconnected to themselves and their strength. They also feel reconnected to their child as a child who is suffering and who needs them, not as a child who is "behaving badly." The exercise allows them to become connected to their creativity that allows them to begin to experience the problem in a new way, be less consumed by it, and be more distanced. This allows them to approach what is happening with more balanced emotions.

References

Siegel, D., & M. Hartzell. (2003). *Parenting from the inside out.* New York: Jeremy Tarcher.

Siegel, D. (1999). *The developing mind: How relationships and the brain interact to shape who we are.* New York: The Guilford Press.

Speert, E. (2000). Personal communication with the author. The Art Therapy Center of North San Diego County, San Diego, CA.

About The Author

Deborah Armstrong Hickey, Ph.D., LMFT, RPT-S, has been licensed as a Marriage and Family Therapist specializing in expressive and play therapies for thirty years. She is a core faculty member at Capella University in Counselor Education and maintains a practice at The Mindgarden in Greenville, South Carolina, where she makes her home. Dr. Hickey is past-president of the California Association for Play Therapy, is currently serving as President of the South Carolina Association for Play Therapy, and sits as a member of the Board of Directors of the International Association for the Study of Dreams. She presents regularly at state, national, and international conferences.

Socio-Sand-Atom
Source: Sheila Ostroff

Theme: Engagement and Assessment
Recommended Age Range: Seven and Up
Treatment Modality: Individual

Goals
- Gather a past and present client history similar to a genogram
- Establish a narrative (concrete and symbolic)
- Externalize personal relationships through the use of spatial placement
- Create a safe place to concretize loss or a traumatic history

Materials
- A variety of individual objects and figurines such as those used in sand play therapy
- A circular tray, 12-16" in diameter. The bottom of plastic planters can be used
- Clean sand to fill the tray
- A Polaroid camera or digital camera/printer for record keeping
- A system to record client information

Description
Ask the client the following three questions:

1. Can you choose one or more objects to represent yourself and place it in the sand in the center of the circle?
2. Can you choose objects to represent people or pets (living or dead) that have been important to you?
3. Can you place these objects around the center, putting the persons you feel close to at the nearest to the center and those you don't feel as close to further away from the center? If scary individuals have been chosen, they can be placed on the outside of the tray.

Observe and assess the details below as the client chooses and places the figurines or objects:
- Where and how are the objects positioned?
- In what directions are the objects facing?
- Whom does the client feel close to or distant from?
- How close to or how far away are they from the client in the center?
- Has the client chosen one or more objects to represent herself/himself?
- How does the client see herself/himself, family members, and friends?
- How many or how few objects are chosen to fill the space?
- What types of objects are chosen?

- What sizes have been chosen for the objects?
- How comfortable is the client working with the symbolic objects?

Process the Socio-Sand-Atom by asking the following questions:

- Can you explain your choices for the Socio-Sand-Atom?
- Who has been represented in the tray?
- Who have you included and why?
- Why have you placed or positioned them in those spaces?
- Is anyone purposely not included, and if so, why not?
- Would you like to choose a figurine for the individual you omitted, but leave it out of the tray?
- Who, what, and where are your support systems?
- Who do you feel close to or distant from?
- Has anyone hurt or traumatized you? (An abuser is to remain out of the tray and possibly covered up.)
- What else do you feel is important to say about your Socio-Sand-Atom?
- How did you feel as you were creating your Socio-Sand-Atom?

At the end of the session a photographic record is taken.

Discussion

This activity is a combination of a social atom, a sand play experience, and a genogram. As a social atom, it is used to show the client relationships and interactions with the individuals that surround her/him in real life. This method introduces the client to a world of sensory, symbolic, and sand play. It is similar to a genogram in that it can be used as a tool to gather personal, family, and social history.

The round tray is purposely suggestive of a mandala, which has been considered by Jungian psychotherapists to be the embodiment of the self.

This assessment method is multidimensional. It can be used as a formative evaluation when beginning with a new client, and once more as a termination assessment. It helps to introduce the concept of symbolic and projective play to the client in a very gentle, engaging way by involving her/him in a playful thought process. It demonstrates how the client envisions herself/himself. It facilitates assessment of the client's family history.

The information the client provides respects the client's pace. It is important not to go beyond what is willingly volunteered.

This is a directive and projective assessment. It links the objects with individuals by externalizing their emotional thought process. Since "thoughts affect feelings," this activity helps the client express underlying problems she/he may be experiencing.

The Socio-Sand-Atom helps the client to begin to tell his/her own story. Comparing multiple trays can also be used to qualitatively evaluate psychological change, through a comparison of previous trays. Upon termination, this comparison allows the client to see the concrete personal changes that have been made.

About the Author
Sheila Ostroff, MA, CCC, CPT, is a certified Canadian counselor, a grief recovery counselor, and an art, sand play and drama psychotherapist. She is trained in trauma psychotherapy, EMDR, and CBT. In her private practice, Sheila sees individuals with ADHD and LD, trauma, and chronic illness, as well as abused children, anxious teens, and mothers at risk. Her professional objective is to help find order and balance in chaos, and to focus on symbolic expression and self-esteem with children. With adults and teens she works on identity and transitional challenges and stress relief.

If I Were a Superhero
Source: Susan Kelsey

Theme: Engagement and Assessment
Recommended Age Range: Six to Ten
Treatment Modality: Individual, Group

Goals
- Assess the client's coping mechanisms
- Improve the client's ability to conquer fears

Materials
- Markers, colored pencils, pencils, or crayons
- Drawing paper
- Lined paper and pen

Description
Explain the activity as follows:

"Let's pretend that you are a Superhero who has never been invented before. Imagine what you look like, what your superpowers are, and how you use them. For instance, Spiderman looks like a spider in a web, is able to climb up buildings and throw webs on people, and he uses his powers to capture mean guys. After you invent your Superhero, draw your Superhero in action on this paper."

After the client finishes her/his drawing, explore in depth who she/he has invented, what the superpowers are and how they are used. Write down each answer on the lined paper. It is also helpful to explore how the Superhero may be like the client.

Discussion
The client's Superhero can provide valuable information about her/his coping strategies. Children who are traumatized or feel helpless may have trouble inventing a Superhero. If this is the case, then this activity can be reintroduced as therapy progresses to assess the child's progress.

About The Author
Susan Kelsey, MS, MFT, RPT-S, is a licensed Marriage and Family Therapist and Registered Play Therapist Supervisor in private practice in Orange County, California. Her practice is limited to children from birth to 18 for nearly all issues related to childhood. Susan is an international speaker and presenter on various topics related to the treatment of children and adolescents. She is currently President of the Orange County Chapter of the California Association of Marriage and Family Therapists and is the founder and past president of the Orange County Chapter of the California Association for Play Therapy.

I Am, I Think I Am, I Don't Think I Am
Source: Susan T. Howson

Theme: Engagement and Assessment
Recommended Age Range: Eight to Fourteen
Treatment Modality: Individual

Goals
- Assess the child's self-esteem and world view
- Discover the positive and negative beliefs the child has of herself/himself
- Increase values vocabulary

Materials
- One set of Manifest Your Magnificence Affirmation Cards for Kids (to order go to www.magnificentcreations.com or call 1-866-511-3411)

Description
The practitioner has the child sort the affirmation cards into three piles: attributes that she/he knows she/he has, attributes she/he thinks she/he has, and attributes that she/he doesn't think she/he has.

The child can be engaged in a discussion around how the cards ended up in different piles. The practitioner can pose such discussions as, "I am curious about the cards you put in each pile. Tell me about how you decided to put them there." "I noticed you don't think you are caring. Tell me about this." This allows the child to express how she/he views herself/himself in a safe environment and shows the practitioner which aspects of self the child identifies with and which she/he doesn't. This information can guide the practitioner in future work, by building on the child's perceived strengths and focusing on areas for personal growth.

Discussion
This exercise engages the client actively and experientially in the process of self-awareness. This is a very telling exercise for the practitioner to begin to understand life from the child's perspective, to gain valuable insight into which values the child sees in herself/himself, and to gain a sense of the child's level of self-esteem.

About The Author
Susan T. Howson, MA, CPCC, CHBC, teaches at Ryerson University in Toronto. She has an MA in Instruction and Special Education, is a Certified Professional Coactive Coach, and is a Certified Human Behavior Consultant. Susan is also a Family and Relationship Systems Coach, an author, a keynote speaker, and a humanitarian-award winner. She has also won the International Coaches Federation PRISM award for the development of the Kids Coaching Connection Program and was a finalist for Canadian Coach of the Year. Susan has developed products (Manifest Your Magnificence Creations) that teach positive values and self-esteem.

What If Game
Source: Donicka Budd

Theme: Engagement and Assessment
Recommended Age Range: Seven to Sixteen
Treatment Modality: Individual, Group

Goals
- Assess client's awareness of feelings
- Increase open communication

Materials
- What If Game question cards (included)
- A wastepaper basket

Advance Preparation
To make the What If Game question cards, photocopy the questions provided below onto cardstock and cut them into cards.

Description
Two players take alternate turns throwing crumpled up paper into the wastepaper basket. If a player succeeds in getting the paper into the basket, she/he picks up a What If card and responds to the question on the card. If the player does not succeed in getting the paper into the basket, the other player can ask that person a question.

Discussion
This activity provides valuable assessment information and facilitates open communication. The activity also helps to build therapeutic rapport. For example, if the practitioner selects the card, "What if your pet could share something about you, what would it say?" The practitioner could respond, "My cat would say I'm the biggest slob in the morning." This response helps the client see the practitioner on a more human level.

About The Author
Donicka Budd, CYW, is a certified Professional Child and Youth Worker with ten years of experience working with vulnerable children, youth, and families. Donicka works as a Family Support Counselor in a children's mental health agency and has led several workshops in the Toronto area. Her innovative, playful

style is illustrative of her work with her clients. She is the author of *Empowering Adolescents to Realize Their Potential: Innovative Activities to Engage the "I Don't Know, I Don't Care" Responsive Youth through Expressive Arts and Play* and creator of her own line of therapeutic games. She currently serves on the Board of Directors of the Canadian Association for Child and Play Therapy.

© Donicka Budd

What If Game
Question Cards

What if someone was thinking about you right now, who might that be?	What if your favorite possession could talk, what would it say about you?	What if your pet could share something about you, what would it say?
What if your life was all in color, what colors would it be?	What if your favorite person spent the day with you, what would she/he say about you?	What if you disagreed with something someone did or said, what could this be about?
What if you could ask anyone a question, what might you want to know?	What if someone could do something nice for you, what would that be?	What if someone wanted to know something about you, what would you tell them?
What if you could speak your mind about anything to anyone, what would you say?	What if you had a magic wand that could change three things in your life, what would those be?	What if no one wanted to play with you, what reason might they have? How might you feel?
What if someone gave you some helpful advice to help you with something, what might they say?	What if you could go back in time, what would be happening right now?	What if someone was thinking about how proud they are of you, who might that be?

© Donicka Budd

36

Inside Hurts and Outside Hurts
Source: Lorie Walton

Theme: Engagement and Assessment
Recommended Age Range: Three to Twelve
Treatment Modality: Individual

Goals
- Gather information about the child's hurtful experiences
- Help the child differentiate between inside hurts (feelings) vs. outside hurts (physical body)
- Increase child's ability to identify and discuss hurts
- Assess the child's coping strategies regarding hurtful experiences

Materials
- Box of different sized Band-Aids (small, medium, large)
- Large piece of mural paper
- Crayola Color Changeable Markers™
- The book *The Hurt* by Teddi Doleski (optional)

Description
Read the book *The Hurt,* which describes an inside emotional hurt. Then tell the child that today she/he will be talking about hurts (big hurts, little hurts, inside hurts, and outside hurts). Tell the child that to do this activity a traced outline of her/his body is needed, and ask the child's permission to trace her/his body. The child's body is traced onto the large piece of mural paper with a marker. Then the different sized Band-Aids are displayed and the practitioner explains to the child that sometimes Band-Aids are used to help hurts feel better. The practitioner asks the child to think of a hurt she/he has had in the past or of one that still exists, if the hurt is a big, medium, or little one, and to choose an appropriately sized Band-Aid. The child is asked to stick the Band-Aid onto the part of her/his outlined body that had the hurt — that is, the head, knee, heart, etc. The child is encouraged to verbally name the hurt, for example, "I fell down when riding my bike and cut my knee." The child is then asked to indicate whether it is an inside hurt (involving feelings) or an outside hurt (physical injury to the body). Using a changeable marker (not the white one), the practitioner then writes what the child says beside the Band-Aid. This exercise is continued by using a Band-Aid for each "hurt" the child mentions.

When finished, the practitioner reviews the outlined body with the Band-Aids and identifies the hurts with the child. Ask the child which hurts still exist and which ones do not. If the hurt no longer exists, then using one of the white changeable markers, the child scribbles over the existing written words. This will change the color of the words. Then using a different color, the child writes down beside the changed hurt who or what helped make the hurt go away. This helps the child to become aware that the hurt has gone away and to feel emotionally empowered by the positive change that has occurred.

As hurts are reviewed, the child may identify hurts that continue to exist. The practitioner can help the child think of ways that may eventually help those hurts go away, and make a list of who or what can help those hurts go away to use as a guide to help the child in future sessions.

Discussion

This activity can help the child openly discuss hurts (physical and emotional) and assess whether the child is able to disclose and discuss past and present hurtful experiences.

Often children who have experienced physical trauma, such as corporal punishment or sexual abuse, have not been able to identify that inside emotional hurts can hurt just as much as, if not more than, physical hurts.

It is important to let the child know that sometimes talking about hurts can be hard to do and that she/he can stop the activity at any time if she/he feels scared, unsure, or worried. It is important to regularly "check in" with the child to ensure she/he is comfortable with continuing.

The practitioner must carefully observe the child to assess coping strategies while doing this activity. For instance, does the child calmly participate during this activity or does the child appear stressed, hypervigilant, distant, dissociative? If the child appears highly stressed or emotionally unable to manage this activity, then the activity should be ended. It is best to end this activity as sensitively as possible but also allow for it to be revisited again at another time. One possible explanation is to say, "Sometimes it is really hard to talk about hurts like this and today seems like it is one of those times. How about we stop for today and try it again on another day?"

About The Author

Lorie Walton, MEd, CPT-S, is a Certified Theraplay® Therapist Trainer Supervisor and the owner and Lead Therapist of Family First Play Therapy Centre Inc. in Bradford, Ontario, a center focused on assisting children and families dealing with attachment, trauma, and emotional issues. In conjunction with her private practice, Lorie is a consultant and Play Therapy Clinical Supervisor for agencies within Ontario and is currently the president of the Canadian Association for Child and Play Therapy (CACPT). She offers workshops on Theraplay®, Attachment and Play Therapy related topics, internship opportunities and supervision to those studying to become certified in Play Therapy and Theraplay®.

School Sucks!
Source: Maxine McCleery Bowden

Theme: Engagement and Assessment
Recommended Age Range: Eight to Sixteen
Treatment Modality: Individual

Goals
- Increase open communication
- Gather information about the client
- Help client gain insight into school frustration

Materials
- A long rectangular sheet of paper
- An assortment of miniature items, including those with positive and negative connotations (for example, fairy, prince, princess, witch, action figures, monsters, assortment of animals)

Description
Divide a long rectangular sheet of paper into as many spaces as the child has been in school plus one (for example, for sixth grade, use 6 spaces plus one more). Write a grade into each space: K, 1, 2, 3, 4, 5, 6 …

Have the child choose a figure from the assortment of miniatures that reminds her/him in some way of each teacher she/he has had. To help the child remember, write down the name of each teacher beginning with the current one.

After the child has picked each figure, have her/him tell you what was picked for each grade level and process with the child what each figure represents for her/him. (See suggestions below.) You can also have the child label each grade level and/or teacher with an adjective, or identify one positive memory and one negative memory about each grade. This can lead to a good conversation about education, specific subjects, and school dynamics. Process questions include:

- I see that you picked _____ for ___ grade. Tell me about that.
- So when did school become stressful, negative, problematic? What do you think happened to make it like that?
- What would you like to be different at school?

Discussion
Many children struggle with feelings of failure and frustration as they proceed through school. At some point they may "give up" and feel like they are "stupid." This activity assesses where things may have started to go wrong for the child.

The practitioner can use this tool to determine if there is some historical event that could have led to a downward spiral at school. Children gain a sense of relief and a new ability to hope when they realize that school failure may be multifaceted and not just because they are "lazy."

About the Author

Maxine McCleery Bowden, MA, is a Marriage and Family Therapist Intern at West End Family Counseling Center in Ontario, California. She was an educator for 20 years and is now a school-based counseling specialist working with children from ages 5 to16. She is President of the San Bernardino Chapter of the California Association of Play Therapists.

Family Quilt
Source: Pam Dyson

Theme: Engagement and Assessment
Recommended Age Range: Four and Up
Treatment Modality: Family

Goals
- Establish a positive and open therapeutic environment
- Assess family dynamics
- Focus on positive aspects of the family

Materials
- White card stock
- Colored pencils
- Markers
- Masking tape
- A patchwork quilt

Advance Preparation
Cut two (four or six inch) squares of card stock for each family member.

Description
Begin by showing the quilt and pointing out the different squares that make up the quilt. Lead into a discussion of how a family is like the quilt in that each family member is unique and brings different things to the family and that they are going to make a family quilt.

Give each family member two quilt squares and instruct them to decorate their squares, using markers, to represent themselves and what they bring to the family. Suggest that they can draw about times they were loving or helpful towards another family member, or they can draw hobbies, favorite foods, music they like, personality traits, and so on. They can also draw favorite times spent together as a family.

After the squares have been completed, turn them upside down and tape them together on the reverse side in the shape of a patchwork quilt. Pause for a moment before slowly turning it over as you say, "I present to you the _____ family quilt." Have family members describe what their squares say about them. Family members may ask questions or make comments about each other's squares.

The practitioner can ask questions such as, "What did you learn about each other?" "What one word describes your family quilt?" "What would someone who didn't know your family learn from looking at your quilt?"

Discussion

Quilts are often made from scraps of fabric taken from discarded clothing of family members. When those scraps are joined together, it creates a picture of the family. This activity is an assessment tool that gives the practitioner a picture of how the family members see themselves. Many families struggle with being able to see that each family member brings unique strengths to the family and that without each member, their family would not be complete. The family quilt enables them to see their family from a new perspective.

Creative expression in family therapy sessions allows all family members to be engaged. Interaction and conversation occurs among the family members while they are decorating their squares. This gives the practitioner an opportunity to observe family dynamics and find answers to such questions as, "Was the family interaction positive or negative?" "Did one family member take charge or was the responsibility of making the quilt shared?"

This activity could be adapted to address issues around grief. The family members could make a quilt with the squares representing their individual memories of the person who died.

About The Author

Pam Dyson, MA, is a provisional licensed professional counselor who practices play therapy is St. Louis, Missouri. She is a family therapist at Child Center-Marygrove, a residential treatment facility for children and adolescents with severe behavioral and emotional problems. Pam also works in private practice, under the supervision of Colleen Biri, Psy.D., providing individual and family counseling. A former early childhood educator, she is a consultant and trainer for early childhood professionals through Missouri's trainer registry, OPEN Initiative.

43

Section Two:
Feelings Expression

Section 2: Feelings Expression

I Am .... Check-In Activity
Source: Tina Luna

Theme: Feelings Expression
Recommended Age Range: Ten and Up
Treatment Modality: Individual, Group

Goals
- Establish a positive and safe therapeutic environment
- Increase open communication
- Gather information about client's feelings and needs
- Increase group cohesion

Materials
- Template (included)
- Pencil or pen
- Glue

Advance Preparation
Photocopy the template on brightly colored paper and cut into strips.

Description
At the beginning of each session, the client/group member completes the sentence "I am ...," according to how she/he feels that day. Or the slip can be filled out however the client wishes to complete the sentence. Examples could be: "I am going to my dad's house today," or "I am excited because I am going to a sleepover tonight," or "I am sad because my mom is sick."

The client's sentence completion is used as a point of departure for further discussion.

Discussion
This is an effective "check-in" activity, especially with clients who do not share easily. It can be helpful to let the client know that if she/he is not feeling comfortable sharing, she/he can keep the "I am ..." to herself/himself and glue the written sentence into the scrapbook. When used in a group, this activity gives the members an opportunity to listen to each other, and gives the members who are quieter a structured time to speak. As the client becomes more engaged in therapy, the sharing may be more detailed.

About The Author
Tina Luna, BASc, is a Child and Youth Counselor. She maintains a private practice and works with children in the school setting. She has an honors degree in Family and Social Relations and is currently enrolled in the Play Therapy Certificate Program with the Canadian Association for Child and Play Therapy.

I Am .... Check-In Activity Template

I am

_____

_____

I am

_____

_____

I am

_____

_____

I am

_____

_____

Click! Emotions and Emotions Bingo
Source: Michelle Cotnoir

Theme: Feelings Expression
Recommended Age Range: Six and Up
Treatment Modality: Individual or Group

Goals
- Increase feelings vocabulary
- Increase ability for verbal and non-verbal expression of feelings
- Increase ability to identify different feelings

Materials
- Mirror
- Digital camera
- Printer
- Legal-size file folder
- Glue
- Tokens
- Prizes

Description
Ask the child to facially express different emotions in front of a mirror, such as being:

Afraid
Angry
Bored
Disgusted
Excited
Frightened
Happy
Hurt
Kind
Sad
Shy
Sneaky
Sorry
Surprised

After practicing the emotions in the mirror, ask the child to hold a facial expression of 6, 9, 10, or 12 different emotions. Take pictures of the different emotions.

After they are printed out, have the child glue her/his pictures onto a legal-size file folder, arranged line by line across the folder to make the Bingo game board. The folder can then be used for a game of Emotions Bingo. A caller announces an emotion and everyone who has a photo of that emotion marks it on her/his folder with a token, and then takes a turn to name something that makes her/him feel that emotion. Before beginning to play, decide on the pattern of the game. For example, you may decide to cover one line of photos in a certain direction (from left to right or right to left). The first person to complete the pattern wins a prize.

Discussion

Identifying emotions can be difficult for many children. Some children miss visual cues that should let them know how others are feeling and they may respond inappropriately. This is an engaging way to help children understand facial expressions and recognize emotions in others.

About The Author

Michelle Cotnoir, MSW, RSW, is a social worker who works in Autism Clinical Services for Child Care Resources in Sudbury, Ontario. She is currently enrolled in the Play Therapy Certificate Program with the Canadian Association for Child and Play Therapy.

Revealing Your Feelings
Source: Sueann Kenney-Noziska

Theme: Feelings Expression
Recommended Age Range: Five and Up
Treatment Modality: Individual, Group, Family

Goals
• Increase feelings vocabulary
• Verbally identify and express feelings
• Increase awareness of normal feelings associated with the client's presenting problems

Materials
• Paper
• Black marker
• Crayola Color Changeable Markers™
• Small candy (i.e., Jolly Ranchers™, Hershey Kisses™) or stickers (optional)

Advance Preparation
Draw various shapes (i.e., squares, circles, triangles, hearts, etc.) on the paper using a black marker. The shapes need to be large enough for feeling words to be written inside. Write a feeling word or the word "Treat" (optional) inside each shape using the invisible marker from the package of Crayola Color Changeable Markers™.

Description
Players take turns coloring a shape with one of the Color Changeable Markers™. Coloring the shape will reveal the feeling previously written inside the shape with the invisible marker. After the feeling has been revealed, the player discusses a time she/he experienced that emotion. If the word "Treat" is revealed, the player selects a piece of candy and discusses a feeling of her/his choice. Stickers can be used instead of candy, if desired.

Discussion
This technique facilitates emotional expression of "hidden" feelings. During the course of the activity, feelings are revealed and processed. This technique allows the practitioner to select specific emotions pertaining to the client's diagnosis, treatment plan, or treatment goals. For example, if the client is experiencing depression, the practitioner can select "depressed," "sad," and "upset" as three of the feelings to write inside the shapes. For an anxious child, the words "anxious," "nervous," and "worried" can be selected. The ability to prescriptively select specific emotions allows clinical discretion to ensure treatment goals are addressed.

Throughout the activity, the practitioner has the opportunity to normalize and validate the emotions discussed by the client. As an additional component, coping skills to manage emotional distress can be identified and discussed. This technique can be modified for any stage of treatment and may focus on general emotions or feelings related to a specific presenting problem.

The use of candy or stickers is an optional part of the intervention, but the prospect of "winning" something during the course of the activity may lower defenses and may incorporate an additional component of playfulness into the technique.

Reference
Kenney-Noziska, S. (2008). *Techniques – techniques – techniques: Play-based activities for children, adolescents, and families.* West Conshohocken, PA: Infinity Publishing.

About The Author
Sueann Kenney-Noziska, MSW, LISW, RPT-S, is a Licensed Independent Social Worker and Registered Play Therapist Supervisor specializing in using play therapy in clinical practice with children, adolescents, and families. She is an author, instructor of play therapy, guest lecturer, and internationally recognized speaker who has trained hundreds of professionals. Sueann is President of Play Therapy Corner, Inc., is actively involved in the play therapy community, and is the author of *Techniques-Techniques-Techniques: Play-Based Activities for Children, Adolescents, & Families.*

The Feelings Wheel Game
Source: Norma Leben

Theme: Feelings Expression
Recommended Age Range: Four and Up
Treatment Modality: Individual, Group, Family

Goals
- Teach 64 feeling words for expression of emotions
- Increase client's ability for verbal and non-verbal expression of feelings
- Help client verbally describe causes for negative feelings before anger outburst to achieve greater self-control

Materials
- The Feelings Wheel Game (available from www.playtherapygames.com)

Advance Preparation
Acquire a Feelings Wheel Game, which includes two game boards, each containing 32 feelings, a glossary of feelings, eight game markers, two dice, and an instructional booklet. A 10-minute DVD is in the deluxe package.

Description
Explain the game as follows:

"This game is called the Feelings Wheel Game. Many people think that feelings are abstract things buried deep in our hearts and brain. We have feelings about most things around us like people, places, and activities. To have the ability to feel is what we're born with, but we're not born with the words to describe them. So, today, we're going to start learning those words so that you can share feelings with your parents, family members, and friends.

Let's take a look at the Game Plan on the back of the game. As beginners, let's begin with Feelings Wheel Board #1, see all the feelings faces? Every time we play this game, we need to make a few decisions. First, are we going to move clockwise or counterclockwise around the Feelings Wheel? (pause) Second, do we use one dice or two? (pause) Third, who wants to take the first turn? (pause) Fourth, which color marker do you choose? (pause) Fifth, which feeling word do you choose to start the game? While you're making up your mind, I'll quickly read out the 32 feelings in case it is difficult for you to read upside down. It's OK not to understand all of them for now. We'll eventually learn them all as we play. Each player has the freedom to begin on any feeling word. For this first time, I propose to go a full circle of all 32 steps. Any questions?

For our first game, let's act out our feelings. If I start on "Happy" and roll a five, I count five spaces clockwise and land on "Confident." OK, this is what I act like when I'm confident! (Other players usually chuckle at the light-hearted exaggeration of acting confident.) If you land on a feeling that you have never experienced, you have the choice to act-out the feeling before or after that one. And, if you keep rolling high numbers and finish first, you may put your marker in the center's Safe Place and watch us finish."

After acting out the feelings of the Feelings Wheel Game (FWG) several times, encourage clients to talk about their own feelings. After the preliminary decisions about choosing clockwise or counterclockwise, etc., explain the next phase of the activity as follows:

"This time we'll play the FWG a little differently. We'll roll the dice and when we land on a feeling, instead of acting it out, we'll share a recent or memorable incident that caused this feeling. I'll go first to show you what I mean."

Discussion
This game enhances the clients feeling vocabulary, and teaches self-control and anger management. Self-control and anger-management cannot be taught without laying the groundwork of helping clients learn about feeling words and the appropriate expressions and gestures that go with them.

Children usually enjoy this game. Even children with short attention spans maintain their interest because they enjoy the different stories behind the feelings.

Reference
Leben, Norma Y. (1992). *The feelings wheel game.* Pflugerville, TX. Morning Glory Treatment Center for Children.

About The Author
Norma Leben, MSW, LCSW, ACSW, RPT-S, CPT-P. Since graduating with a University of Chicago MSSA, she has worked as a CPS supervisor, school dropout team leader, residential treatment supervisor, executive director, and international trainer. She is a licensed clinical social worker and Play Therapy Supervisor who has authored over 45 audio or video recordings, books, and publications in English and Chinese on parenting and play therapy techniques.

The Sound of Feelings
Source: Susan T. Howson

Theme: Feelings Expression
Recommended Age Range: Five and Up
Treatment Modality: Individual, Group

Goals
- Increase client's ability for verbal and non-verbal expression of feelings
- Help children begin to understand how to manage feelings more effectively

Materials
- Large ice cream tubs (one per child)
- Construction paper
- Scissors
- Glue
- Stickers
- Markers

Advance Preparation
Empty and clean the ice cream tubs.

Description
Children are given an ice cream tub to decorate however they wish. The practitioner then explains that they are going to use the tubs as drums to show "how different feelings sound."

Have the children drum to different feelings. For example, the practitioner might say, "Show me what feeling angry sounds like on your drum" or "Show me how feeling sad sounds like on your drum." For homework, have the children take the drums home and use them.

Discussion
This activity facilitates the expression of feelings in a non-verbal manner. Children become more aware of their feelings, learn how to recognize a feeling as it happens, and when it is called forth. This activity gives children the opportunity to monitor their feelings in the moment, which is crucial for psychological insight and self-understanding, the keystones of emotional intelligence. Children will enjoy making sounds to identify their different feelings.

About The Author
Susan T. Howson, MA, CPCC, CHBC, teaches at Ryerson University in Toronto. She has an MA in Instruction and Special Education, is a Certified Professional

Coactive Coach, and is a Certified Human Behavior Consultant. Susan is also a Family and Relationship Systems Coach, an author, a keynote speaker, and a humanitarian-award winner. She has also won the International Coaches Federation PRISM award for the development of the Kids Coaching Connection Program and was a finalist for Canadian Coach of the Year. Susan has developed products (Manifest Your Magnificence Creations) that teach positive values and self-esteem.

© Susan T. Howson

Colors of Feelings
Source: Kathryn A. Markell and Marc A. Markell

Theme: Feelings Expression
Recommended Age Range: Four to Eight
Treatment Modality: Individual or Group

Goals
- Verbally identify and express feelings
- Allow children to depict how they are feeling in a concrete manner by using color

Materials
- Large sheets of paper
- Markers or crayons
- The book *Charlotte's Web* by E.B. White (New York: HarperCollins, 2001), optional

Description
Trace the child's body on a large sheet of paper. Ask the child to color the body to represent how she/he feels when she/he is upset. (This question can be made more specific for children dealing with a particular issue. For example, the practitioner might say, "Color the body to show how you feel when you think about your loved one's death.") The child may decide to focus on one part of the body or color the entire body one color or different colors. The child can then explain the color choices.

Next, trace the child's body on a large sheet of paper again. This time, have the child color the body to represent how he/she feels when she/he is not upset. Ask the child to talk about the colors and discuss how she/he might get from the upset colors to the colors that are not upset. The practitioner may want to give an example, "If I had my body traced, and I was going to color part of it to show the color of how I feel, I would color my head brown and green and red. The reason I would color my head these colors is because when I am upset, I feel like I am thinking of so many different things at the same time, and it is confusing. What part of your body might you color when you are upset?" Have the child discuss this question. If the child still has difficulty understanding the activity, the practitioner might ask some specific questions, such as, "How does your heart feel and what color goes with that feeling?" or, "How do your arms feel when you are angry? What color or colors do you think they would be?"

Discussion
Children often have difficulty verbalizing their distress. They may not be able to

verbalize their feelings in words. It may be easier and less threatening for them to express their feelings by using colors.

This activity appears in *The Children Who Lived,* written by the authors (and referenced below) as an exercise to be used in conjunction with reading and discussing *Charlotte's Web* by E.B. White. In the book, Wilbur feels very upset when Charlotte dies. He talks with some of his friends about how upset he feels. Some people may not be able to express how they feel in words like Wibur does. Children may be able to express their upset by using colors.

This activity can also be used as a stand-alone activity; that is, the children would not necessarily need to have read or even talked about *Charlotte's Web.* They could talk about how being upset makes them feel and about how different colors might express how they feel.

Reference
Markell, Kathryn A., and Marc A. Markell. (2008). *The children who lived: Using Harry Potter and other fictional characters to help grieving children and adolescents.* New York: Routledge.

About The Authors
Kathryn A. Markell, Ph.D., teaches child and adolescent psychology at Anoka-Ramsey Community College in Coon Rapids, Minnesota, and researches and writes in the area of grief and loss.

Marc A. Markell, Ph.D., CT, is a professor at St. Cloud State University in St. Cloud, Minnesota. He teaches courses, presents workshops, facilitates grief groups, and researches and writes in the area of grief and loss.

Fishing for Feelings
Source: Sara McCool

Theme: Feelings Expression
Recommended Age Range: Eight to Twelve
Treatment Modality: Individual, Family, Group

Goals
- Increase ability to appropriately identify and express emotions
- Increase knowledge and use of healthy coping skills

Materials
- Magnetic play fishing pole (can be purchased in toy stores)
- Magnetic tape or magnetic paper (available at craft or office supply stores)
- Thin markers
- Index cards
- Scissors
- Brown paper bag
- Bag of Pepperidge Farm Goldfish™
- Small prize

Advance Preparation
Cut two index cards into eight equal pieces. Attach a small piece of magnetic tape or magnetic paper to the back of each of the sixteen pieces of index cards. On the other side of each index card, draw a circle. Place sixteen Goldfish™ in a bag and select a small prize appropriate for the client.

Description
The practitioner explains to the child that they will be making a game for them to play together. The practitioner asks the child to say as many feelings words as she/he can think of, and the practitioner writes one feeling word on each index card (beneath the circle). If the child runs out of feelings words before all sixteen pieces of index cards are filled, the practitioner can help the child by acting out a feeling and having the child guess what the feeling is.

Once sixteen feelings words have been identified and written on the cards, the practitioner asks the child to give eight cards to herself/himself and eight cards to the practitioner. The child and practitioner then draw what they think people look like when they feel that way in each corresponding circle.

Once the cards are ready, the child mixes them up and scatters them on the floor with the magnetic side showing. The child and practitioner take turns "fishing for feelings" by using the magnetic fishing pole. Once a "feeling" is "caught," the "fisherman" is given a chance to earn a Goldfish™. If the fisherman talks about a time they experienced that feeling, they earn one Goldfish™ and they place that feeling card in the brown paper bag. The fisherman can choose to "throw it back" into the pile of feelings, but loses her/his turn.

Once all sixteen cards have been used, the child counts how many feelings (fish) she/he caught. If she/he caught at least eight, the child earns the prize.

Discussion

Many children have a limited emotional vocabulary. This game provides an engaging way to increase their ability to identify a variety of emotions. The Goldfish™ and small prize provide positive reinforcement of expression of emotions.

This game can be modified in a variety of ways. For example, fishermen can earn an extra Goldfish™ if they are able to come up with an appropriate coping skill for the feeling they "catch." The game can be used in family therapy, with players sharing a time they felt the feeling in interactions with other family members. The game can also be tailored to specific treatment issues - for example, "Tell about a time you had this feeling during your parents' divorce."

About The Author

Sara McCool, MSW, LCSW, RPT, is a social worker and Registered Play Therapist in Terre Haute, Indiana. She is the founder of the Child Empowerment Center, a private practice that serves children, adolescents, and their families. Her work focuses on treating abused and neglected children and their caregivers. She enjoys working with other play therapists on the Board of Directors of the Indiana Association for Play Therapy, and is currently serving as President-Elect.

Guess Who? Feelings Game
Source: Kimberly Blackmore

Theme: Feelings Expression
Recommended Age Range: Six and Up
Treatment Modality: Individual

Goals
- Identify, label, and express a variety of feelings
- Increase awareness of various feeling states
- Identify the connection between feelings and facial features
- Strengthen the therapeutic relationship

Materials
- Feeling faces (feeling faces are drawn by the client and the practitioner)
- Guess Who? Game™
- Blue and red pieces of cardboard
- Markers
- Scissors
- Glue stick

Advance Preparation
Make two sets of the feeling faces (total of 48 face cards), color each face, and slide each face into a different face frame provided by the Guess Who? Game.™ A third set of 24 feeling faces needs to be prepared to be used as the mystery feeling face cards.

The identical feeling face cards need to be colored in a similar fashion so that each player can guess the feelings by identifying facial expressions as well as hair, eye, or skin color.

Description
The practitioner explains to the child that they are going to play a game about feelings. The child and practitioner each choose either a blue or red piece of cardboard to use as a game board. All faces in the frame need to be flipped upright. The mystery feeling cards are shuffled and placed face down on the table. The child and practitioner each choose at random one mystery feeling card. This card is placed in the face card slot so that the mystery feeling card faces that player.

The objective of the game is to guess the other player's mystery feeling face before they guess yours. On your turn, ask the other player one question and eliminate any game board feeling faces that don't fit the mystery feeling face description. Notice the differences among the 24 feeling faces on your game board. Ask questions about hair, eye, or skin color; some faces can have beards, some can be wearing hats or glasses. Also have the child notice that each face is expressing a different emotion.

Each question must be a "yes" or "no" answer. For example, does your person have the corners of their mouth turning up? Does your person have red hair? The other player must then answer "yes" or "no." When you are ready to guess who the mystery feeling face is, make your guess on your turn. The other player must then tell you whether or not your guess is correct.

The practitioner can bring to the child's attention the connection between the feeling and the facial features by modeling the emotion. The child is then asked to mimic the expression of the affect while looking in a mirror. The practitioner may also encourage the child to provide an example of when she/he may have experienced that emotion.

Discussion
This game helps children identify, label, and express a variety of emotions. Since most children enjoy playing board games, they will find this activity engaging and it will help to strengthen the therapeutic rapport.

About The Author
Kimberly Blackmore, M.C., is a Play Therapy Intern with Branching Out Therapeutic Services in Brampton, Ontario. Kimberly specializes in working with children living in therapeutic foster homes or group-home settings who are experiencing a variety of emotional and behavioral difficulties. She provides individual play therapy, co-facilitates groups for children and teens, as well as individual assessments. She has completed the Canadian Association for Child and Play Therapy (C.A.C.P.T.) Certificate Program.

Connect 4 and Oh So Much More
Source: Cynthia A. Dodge

Theme: Feelings Expression
Recommended Age Range: Six to Adult
Treatment Modality: Individual, Family

Goals
- Maintain optimal levels of arousal. This includes possibility of either increasing tolerance for arousal and emotion (i.e., up-regulation), or decreasing general level of arousal (i.e., down-regulation)
- Internalize an awareness of how the body feels at different states of arousal

Materials
- Connect 4 Board Game™
- Post-it® Notes colorful quarter-size diameter dots
- Emoticons Reference Guide
- Markers
- Small spiral-bound notebook
- Pink powder puff

Description
The game of Connect 4 serves as the foundation for this technique. Players choose the color of chip they wish to claim as their own. The child is asked to draw feeling emoticon faces on the Post-it® sticker dots. (Having a reference guide to sample eases this component.) The dots are placed on the child's chosen color discs. As each face is completed, the practitioner engages in a dialog and queries and/or describes the emotion that best corresponds to that representation. Either the practitioner or child transfers the represented face/emotion image by hand into the spiral-bound notebook with a defined feeling and brief description of that feeling or situation in which the feeling occurs.

Once all the corresponding chips are decorated, Connect 4 is played according to the traditional rules. At the onset of the game, the practitioner uses this mantra to introduce play: "Connect 4 and so much more. When it's done, it's out the door." The "out the door" phrase refers to the release of the chips upon the successful completion of the game.

The approach to the game differs according to the child's need for regulation. If the child is lethargic, disinterested, detached, or removed and distant, the practitioner projects enthusiasm, joy, and buoyancy through a chant that references the dropping of the chip into the structure, "Kerplunk, Kerplunk, Elbow Dunk" and works to engage the child to give an elbow to elbow connection.

If the child is anxious, unsettled, distractible, hyperactive, or inattentive, the clinician quietly whispers at each chip drop, "Kerplink, kerplink, powder puff pink," and gently strokes the forearm, the back of the hand, or the cheek of the client with the pink powder puff.

The player who has successfully connected 4 same color chips wins. These emoticons serve as the basis to create a cohesive story. If the child has won and is hesitant, the practitioner creates the first story, all the while encouraging the child to make her/his own corrections, additions, or story rendition. Praise for the attempt and creation of a feeling story is very much integral to the mastery component of this technique. The winner's face story is then recorded in the spiral-bound notebook that has the child's name on it for future reference.

Discussion

Children who have experienced trauma or have attachment-related issues are often disconnected from or unaware of their own emotional experience. They may be unable to identify and differentiate between emotions, have a lack of awareness of their own body, and have a reduced capacity to connect these states to the event(s) that triggers them. This activity weaves these fundamental concepts together in a manner that will encourage mastery of these very crucial emotion management skills in a challenging, engaging, and fun manner.

Repeatedly playing this game can result in a compilation of many feeling states that become woven together in a playful way with a regulated arousal state associated with various affective states. Integrating a positive psycho-educational frame into this experience further solidifies the attainment of mastery. The practitioner might conclude by saying to the child, "You managed to discuss how mad, anxious, silly, and sad related to a story with a relaxed body and a gentle tone. You are taking charge of yourself by doing that. If you can discuss those feelings through a game and with me, you can also do it by listening to your body at other times."

About The Author

Cynthia A. Dodge, Ph.D., LCSW, RPT-S, holds a degree in counseling psychology, is a licensed clinical social worker, and a registered play therapy supervisor in Portland, Maine, where she is the director of clinical services for a large community mental health agency. Cynthia is the co-author of *The Anger Addict*, a contributor to *101 More Favorite Play Therapy Techniques*, and a featured columnist for *Parent & Family* newspaper and the e-zine *Good Health New England*.

Roll That Emotion
Source: Michelle Cotnoir

Theme: Feelings Expression
Recommended Age Range: Eight to Thirteen
Treatment Modality: Individual, Group

Goals
- Increase feelings vocabulary
- Increase ability for verbal and non-verbal expression of feelings
- Increase ability to identify different feelings

Materials
- Emotion Dice and Visual Emotion Dice (included)
- Tape
- Cue card (included)

Advance Preparation
Emotion Dice: Photocopy the Emotion Dice template and cut the outline shape. Fold into a box to create a cube. Tape the sides together to create an Emotion Dice. The dice will be sturdier if it is laminated before folding it into a box and taping the sides together.

Visual Emotion Dice: Photocopy the Visual Emotion Dice template and cut the outline shape. Fold into a box to create a cube. Tape the sides together to create a Visual Emotion Dice. The dice will be sturdier if it is laminated before folding it into a box and taping the sides together.

Photocopy the cue card template and cut it out.

Description
Emotion Dice: Each person, including the practitioner, takes a turn rolling the dice. The other players close their eyes so they cannot see which emotion has been rolled. The emotion that the player rolls is the emotion that she/he must act out visually for the audience. In turn, the audience must guess the emotion. For example, if a player rolls the dice and it turns up "sad," then she/he must act out "sad" without using words.

Visual Emotion Dice: Each person, including the practitioner, takes a turn rolling the dice. The player must talk about a time when she/he felt the emotion that was just rolled. For example, if the player rolls the dice and it turns up "sad," then she/he must talk about a time when she/he felt sad. The player can be prompted with a cue card.

Discussion

Emotion Dice: This activity can be used when children have difficulties in the area of emotion recognition. We learn about people's thoughts and feelings by their emotional expressions. Specifically, emotions are revealed through facial expressions, voice, and gestures. This activity helps children to identify various emotional states in themselves and in others.

Visual Emotion Dice: This activity can be used when children are having difficulties expressing their emotions. It helps them to clearly define and name a feeling, while relating it to a particular event.

About The Author

Michelle Cotnoir, MSW, RSW, is a social worker who works in Autism Clinical Services for Child Care Resources in Sudbury, Ontario. She is currently enrolled in the Play Therapy Certificate Program with the Canadian Association for Child and Play Therapy.

Roll That Emotion: Emotion Dice

Roll That Emotion: Cue Card

1. When?
2. Where?
3. What happened?
4. How did your body feel? Tummy, head, hands, other?
5. What did you do?

Healing Hangman
Source: Cherilyn Rowland Petrie

Theme: Feelings Expression
Recommended Age Range: Ten to Adolescent
Treatment Modality: Individual, Group

Goals
- Build therapeutic rapport and increase client engagement
- Decrease resistance to discussing feelings and other topics
- Create opportunities to teach clients coping and other skills
- Increase cooperation and cohesion in group format

Materials
- Dry erase board and markers

Description
The practitioner presents the familiar childhood game of Hangman as the session activity and explains that instead of one word being chosen, a whole sentence will be used in each turn. The practitioner will then draw the gallows and use dashed lines to represent each word in the sentence, clearly separating each word from the others. In a group format, each client is encouraged to guess a letter and/or discuss possible solutions for the puzzle. After the puzzle has been solved, the clients will have to respond to the message on the board and discuss the topic. A didactic approach can be used at this point if clients are unfamiliar with the subject matter. Clients are encouraged to take turns as well, creating a puzzle for either the practitioner or the other group members to solve.

Sample Puzzles for Engagement and Rapport Building:
- Tell me three important things about you.
- Share a memory of your favorite vacation.
- What do you like to do for fun?

Sample Puzzles for Addressing Feelings:
- Share a time you felt angry.
- Talk about something that made you feel excited.
- What is something you do to feel better?

Sample Puzzles for Other Topics:
- (Social Skills) What are three qualities you look for in a good friend?
- (Trauma) Share your thoughts on why this happened to you.
- (Self-Esteem) Name three things you like about yourself.

Discussion

Many children and adolescents are uncomfortable talking and answering specific questions about sensitive topics. They find it easier to become engaged when involved in game play. Modifying the structure of a familiar game will encourage them to more readily participate and will help them more easily share in the rhythm of communication, making it easier for them to open up about feelings. The use of whole sentences is also important for client engagement, as most clients will be able to solve puzzles fairly easily and will not become discouraged by failure. Early in the therapeutic relationship, less emotionally intense puzzles may be used, while latter games may be more targeted and powerful. A puzzle's theme can be very specific for an individual client to help address her/his unique needs and circumstances. This approach can be broadened to include topics about social skills, boundaries, traumatic experiences, self-esteem, and termination issues.

About The Author

Cherilyn Rowland Petrie holds an MA in Clinical Psychology and is a Licensed Mental Health Counselor practicing in the State of Florida. She provides trauma-focused therapy for children and families as part of Kids House of Seminole, a children's advocacy center. She has also given lectures regarding phase-oriented treatment models for sexual trauma survivors, compassion fatigue, and play therapy with dissociative disorders.

Call It Out
Source: Cherilyn Rowland Petrie_

Theme: Feelings Expression
Recommended Age Range: Nine to Sixteen
Treatment Modality: Group

Goals
- Increase clients engagement in group activity
- Decrease clients resistance to discussing feelings and other topics
- Create opportunities to teach clients coping and other skills
- Increase cooperation and cohesion in group format

Materials
- Game cards, printed on card stock (sample cards for sexual trauma work are included)

Description
The group leader presents this variation of the game Outburst™ and explains that in this game teams choose a card based on a category and then must shout out as many possible answers as they can. One point is awarded for each answer appearing on the card held by the practitioner. Points are totaled throughout the session. The team with the most points wins once all the cards are played. Each topic card has 10 possible responses. When playing in teams, there needs to be an equal number of topic cards available.

Optional variations include allotting points for excellent answers not appearing on the cards or allowing a second-chance round for the second team to guess answers missed by the first team during its turn at that particular topic. Teams may also be given specific time limitations for guessing.

Topic cards can be adapted for almost any topic, including domestic violence, bereavement, divorce, behavior problems, or anger management. Topic cards can be left intentionally blank to encourage clients to share their unique experiences, such as what triggers negative memories or what they might miss about a lost loved one. In these cases, points are awarded for any response they give; although clients are unaware this is being done.

Discussion
Many children and adolescents are uncomfortable talking and answering specific questions about sensitive topics. They find it easier to engage when involved in game play. By modifying the structure of a familiar game, they readily participate and view participation as play instead of therapeutic work. Group members are willing to share

more openly in this type of format. This game can address feelings, beliefs about their situation, coping skills, and information on needed skills while encouraging team interaction and bonding.

About The Author

Cherilyn Rowland Petrie holds an MA in Clinical Psychology and is a Licensed Mental Health Counselor practicing in the State of Florida. She provides trauma-focused therapy for children and families as part of Kids House of Seminole, a children's advocacy center. She has also given lectures regarding phase-oriented treatment models for sexual trauma survivors, compassion fatigue, and play therapy with dissociative disorders.

Note: Barrett Williams, MA, contributed to the Call It Out Sexual Abuse Card set.

Call It Out Game Cards
(Sexual Abuse Version)

Feelings after Abuse
1. Angry
2. Sad
3. Confused
4. Scared
5. Different
6. Hopeless
7. Yucky
8. Guilty
9. Ashamed
10. Numb

After-Effects of Abuse
1. Nightmares
2. Flashbacks
3. Poor self-esteem
4. Poor boundaries
5. Trouble making decisions
6. Depression
7. Anxiety
8. Anger
9. Bad grades/bad behavior
10. Trouble concentrating

Thoughts after Abuse
1. I'm bad
2. I'm not good enough
3. It's my fault
4. I got (the offender) in trouble
5. I'm different
6. I'm dirty/damaged
7. Things will never get better
8. Everyone will know
9. I can't say no
10. This is all I'm good for

Impact of Abuse on Family
1. Financial problems
2. Separation/relocation
3. Guilt
4. Role confusion
5. Scape-goating
6. Legal case
7. Everybody is upset
8. Distrust of each other
9. Mixed feelings
10. Parents don't understand

Defenses
1. Avoidance
2. Denial
3. Not talking about it
4. Emotional numbing/guarding
5. Acting out
6. Hiding behind anger
7. Minimizing
8. Controlling
9. Escaping through activity
10. Sarcasm/humor

Offender's Threats
1. I will hurt you
2. I will hurt your family
3. Nobody will believe you
4. I will tell people you wanted it
5. Your mother will abandon you
6. You will make me get in trouble
7. You will destroy the family
8. Your mother already knows
9. I know where you live
10. Physical threat, non-verbal

Call It Out Game Cards
(Sexual Abuse Version)

Offender's Tricks and Manipulations
1. Gives gifts/bribes
2. Gives extra attention
3. Separates/isolates
4. Controls by lies
5. Keeps secrets
6. Makes you believe it's your fault
7. Threatens violence
8. Offers alcohol/drugs
9. Progressive boundary violations
10. Claims it's teaching/helping

Offender's Excuses
1. I didn't do it
2. She/he's lying
3. She/he wanted it
4. Sex education
5. She/he seduced me
6. We were just playing
7. It was consensual
8. I thought you were your mother
9. I couldn't help myself
10. I was a victim of abuse

Not Guilty!
1. You were a child
2. You couldn't defend yourself
3. They were bigger/stronger
4. Sexual abuse is a crime
5. All children like attention
6. Children follow rules/adults
7. You trusted them
8. It's hard to act when scared
9. They made the decision
10. Adults can manipulate children

Healthy Relationships
1. Consenting
2. Equal
3. Respectful
4. Trusting
5. Safe
6. Listens to you
7. Good limits/boundaries
8. Helps/encourages you
9. Honest
10. Values your input

Coping Skills
1. Deep breathing
2. Writing/journaling
3. Walking/exercise/sports
4. Talking it out
5. Artwork/drawing
6. Throwing a ball at the wall
7. Listening to music
8. Reading/learning
9. Self-talk
10. Grounding skills

Safety Skills
1. Tell until you are believed
2. Know what to do and when
3. Trust your instincts
4. Don't trust blindly
5. Pay attention to people
6. Pay attention to situations
7. Have a safety plan
8. Know who to tell
9. Stop and think
10. Be ready to ask for help

Telling, Guessing, and Listening Game
Source: Mary Cowper-Smith

Theme: Feelings Expression
Recommended Age Range: Six and Up
Treatment Modality: Family (Two or more family members are required)

Goals
- Increase open communication among family members
- Assist the family in positive, playful interaction
- Identify positive aspects of family life and areas for change

Materials and Advance Preparation
- 18" x 18" piece of bristol board on which are drawn about 100 rectangles (1" wide by 1.5" long) joined to make a winding path from Go in the lower-left corner to Finish in the upper-right corner of the board. Color the first rectangle pink, the next one yellow, and on the third write the words "Roll again." Repeat this pattern through to Finish. (If using the variation described below, color a few spaces green.)
- Playing pieces for each participant
- Dice
- Twenty each of pink and yellow index cards (about 3" x 5"), on which are written sentence stubs (see below). Place the piles of pink and yellow cards face down beside the game board.
- Small candies or chips

Description
Explain the game as follows:

"The first player rolls the dice and moves the playing piece the indicated number of spaces on the board. If the player lands on a pink rectangle, she/he picks up the first pink card and reads the sentence stub aloud. If she/he chooses to complete the sentence, she/he receives a candy. The player on her/his left then takes a turn, and so on around the board. If a player lands on a yellow space, she/he picks up the yellow card on the top of the pile and reads the sentence stub aloud. She/he then thinks of the answer, but does not share it with the other players. The player who is able to guess the answer receives the candy. The game continues until one or more players reaches Finish (or until the desired time for the game is finished.)"

Play is interspersed with conversations, facilitated by the practitioner, to encourage a deeper level of disclosure of feelings and ideas, to invite responses from other participants, to support risk-taking, and to ensure that family members are hearing each other accurately.

Variations
The board may be constructed with occasional green rectangles interspersed among the pink, yellow, and white ones. Short instructions for relaxation are

written on green cards. When a player lands on a green space, she/he reads the instruction aloud, and all players take a short break to complete the recommended exercise.

At a second or third session of this game, players are given blank pink index cards on which to write their own questions or sentence stubs for the other players. The practitioner also contributes cards. The practitioner then mixes the cards written by the participants in with the ones written by the practitioner. When a player lands on a pink space, the practitioner reads aloud the question or sentence stub in order to prevent participants from observing the handwriting and attributing the question to a family member. Participants are thus given an opportunity to ask their own questions without having their identity revealed. (This idea was contributed by Laurie Stein, MSW, RSW.)

Sample sentence stubs for pink cards:
    One thing about _____ that makes me proud is _____.
    I feel close to my (mother, father, son, daughter) when _____.
    I feel hurt when _____.
    I feel safe and comfortable when _____.

Sample sentence stubs for yellow cards (these are more playful):
    One way I can be sure of ticking off my (brother, sister, father, mother, daughter, son) is to _____.
    My most comfortable clothes are _____.
    My favorite time of day is _____.
    My favorite flavor of ice cream is _____.

Discussion

The purpose of this game is to increase open communication among family members, especially in situations where children require support to express their feelings to their parents or siblings or when family members would benefit from an opportunity to hear positive comments from the others. If children are particularly worried about a parent's reaction to their feelings or comments, it may be necessary to begin the session with a discussion of this concern, eliciting assurance from the parent that anything shared in the game will not result in negative repercussions at home. At the completion of the game, it may be useful to talk with the family about what they have learned about each other that is new and surprising, and about their new understandings of, and reaction to, other members' feelings and perspectives. They may also benefit from discussion about how they will go about expanding the positive aspects of family life that have been identified, and implementing any changes in the family that have been requested.

About The Author

Mary Cowper-Smith, MSW, RSW, has been employed as a social worker in London and Stratford, Ontario, and in Goose Bay and St. John's, Newfoundland. She currently works with separating, divorcing, and remarrying families at Families in Transition, Family Services Toronto.

The Image Finds Words
Source: Lysa Toye

Theme: Feelings Expression
Recommended Age Range: Nine and Up
Treatment Modality: Group, Family

Goals
- Explore concepts, beliefs, and associations related to a word ("death" or any other topic one wishes to explore in the group such as divorce, family, sadness, etc.)
- Increase group/family cohesion

Materials
- Paper
- Markers or crayons
- Pen

Description
The practitioner introduces the activity by asking group participants to take paper and drawing materials of their choice and draw an image of whatever comes to mind when they hear the word "death" (other words can be used to explore other personal concepts). Group members are told that the image can be representational or abstract, and may relate to an abstract idea of death, to a personal experience they have had, or stories they have heard about others' experiences of death. They should be instructed that these images will be shared with the group; for groups new to artwork or shy about sharing, the members should be reassured that there is no wrong way to create their images.

When the images are completed, group members lay them out in a circle; clean sheets of paper are placed beside them. The group is asked to move around the circle, to look at each image that has been created, and to write down on the clean sheet of paper a word or phrase that they feel when they look at each of the images. All group members should thus offer a response to each image other than their own.

When everyone has given a written response, group members return to their own image and look at the responses, keeping in mind that others may have very different associations with the image than they do or construe a different meaning. Members are asked to get a clean piece of paper and writing materials of their choice and to then use the words or phrases they have been "given" as the skeleton for a poem about death (or other concept). They can add words or leave out words that they have been given, but they can be guided by the responses

74

provided by the others in the group.

When group members have completed their poems, they are invited to read them aloud to the group as well as showing the group the image they created.

Discussion
Many children, adolescents, and adults benefit from creative explorations of their ideas and associations about their experiences, but feel shy or have difficulty entering into a creative means of exploring them. This activity provides an accessible, non-evaluative entry into expressive modalities and non-linear explorations of concepts and associations in a shared, interactive environment. Individuals are given "feedback" on their unique creations in a way that is supportive and less threatening, and they are given control about how to use that feedback to build on their own experience and understanding. This exercise also demonstrates the power of shifting between modalities to deepen exploration and redirect play, and offers an introduction to shared images in the group environment. Children and adults alike are often surprised at their "skill" in the arts, which allows them to open creative spaces for different expressive modalities.

About The Author
Lysa Toye, MSW, RSW, Dip. EXAT, is an expressive arts therapist and social worker with a collaborative certificate in Palliative and Supportive Care from the University of Toronto. She works at the Max and Beatrice Wolfe Centre for Children's Grief and Palliative Care at the Temmy Latner Centre for Palliative Care, Mount Sinai Hospital, where she provides psychosocialspiritual support and education for children and their families living with the experience of dying and death through illness, accident and other traumatic means. Lysa studied expressive arts therapy at ISIS-Canada and the European Graduate School and has studied and created art through drawing and painting, ceramics, movement, voice, poetry and play. She believes in the power of creativity, play, art, ritual and the natural world to ground us in and awaken us to the full experience of being human.

People I Like
Source: Lisa Stein

Theme: Feelings Expression
Recommended Age Range: Eight and Up
Treatment Modality: Individual

Goals
- Identify qualities the client appreciates in others
- Identify the limitations of others
- Increase the client's awareness of her/his personal strengths
- Gather information about the client's support network

Materials
- A whiteboard and markers or large sheet of paper and markers
- Paper cut outs of human figures

Description
Ask the client which qualities she/he would seek out in choosing a friend. These are listed on the paper or whiteboard. The client can then choose a color for each quality. The practitioner then reviews the important people in the client's life: friends, family, athletic coaches, teachers, etc. Younger children can then write a person's name on a cut out and color it in according to which qualities they possess, and in what proportion. Older children may prefer to draw a pie chart for the perceived qualities of each person, or assign percentages to a person — that is, a client's mother may get 20% loving, 30% kind, 10% reliable, etc. Not everyone will possess the same qualities or in the same proportion. The practitioner can then ask the client to chart herself/himself and perhaps the practitioner as well.

Discussion
This intervention lends itself to a rich exploration of the client's perceptions of others, and of herself/himself. Children tend to see others in black and white terms, and if this is the case, it will become evident during the process. Even older children and teens can be confused by the inconsistencies in other people. This intervention can contribute to a more sophisticated and tolerant view of others. Children can come to appreciate the qualities of others while understanding that we all have limitations. For example, the client may seek out one individual for their compassion, but another for their sense of humor. This activity can also be used to explain why it may be beneficial to forgive someone when they disappoint, as opposed to ending the relationship, as that person may still have much to offer in other ways.

This intervention may also be used to identify those in a child's life whom she/he can rely on in safety situations as they may be "reliable," "helpful," "caring," etc. This exercise may give the child a greater understanding of her/his own strengths and what she/he may have to offer others that is of value; this in turn addresses the client's self-esteem.

About The Author

Lisa Stein, MA is in private practice in Toronto. She works with children, teens, adults, and couples. Lisa has completed the Play Therapy Certificate program through the Canadian Association for Child and Play Therapy and is also trained in EMDR.

Power Pies
Source: Kim L. Flournoy

Theme: Feelings Expression
Recommended Age Range: Nine to Sixteen
Treatment Modality: Individual, Group

Goals
- Increase open communications about power dynamics within the family
- Validate the client's feelings of power imbalance within the family

Materials
- 3 sheets of plain paper
- Markers (various colors)

Description
The practitioner engages the child in a discussion regarding the concept of sharing. The practitioner discusses cutting and serving a pie for dessert and asks how big or small of a slice each member of the family (1) thinks she/he should get? (2) actually gets. (3) the child wishes they got.

The practitioner asks the child to define power. The practitioner then introduces the concept of power in families (that is, decision-making, discipline, etc.) and asks the child to share her/his perspective of power within the family.

The practitioner directs the child to draw one circle, or pie, on each sheet of plain paper. Using different colors to represent each member of the family, the practitioner prompts the child to "slice up the Power Pie" first showing the size each member of the family thinks she/he should get. On the second pie, the practitioner prompts the child to "slice up the Power Pie" showing the size each member of the family tends to actually get. On the third pie, the practitioner prompts the child to "slice up the Power Pie" showing the size the child wishes each family member got.

The practitioner and child line up the three Power Pies on a table. The practitioner facilitates further dialogue about the child's perceptions of the child's family dynamics, the reality of the child's family dynamics, and the child's wishes for her/his family dynamics.

Discussion
This activity provides an opportunity for clients to express power dynamics in their family. The "slicing of the Power Pie" gives the clients the chance to express feelings, as well as the practitioner the chance to assess the client.

Power Pies can also be used in family work by having each member of the family do this activity, then comparing each member's perceptions of power with other family members.

About The Author
Kim L. Flournoy, MSW, is the Director of Children's Services for Safe Harbor, a comprehensive domestic violence program. She was the first recipient of the Virginia Sexual and Domestic Violence Action Alliance's Blue Ribbon Award for excellence in children's advocacy. She developed and taught an international distance-learning course on play therapy. She serves on numerous boards and committees related to trauma and children. As a freelance consultant, she provides training on child trauma, play therapy, and vicarious trauma.

Heartfelt Feelings Coloring Cards Strategies
Source: David A. Crenshaw

Theme: Feelings Expression
Recommended Age Range: Six to Twelve for the expressive domain; Nine to Twelve for the relational domain
Treatment Modalities: Individual, Group, Family

Goals
- Teach feelings and vocabulary of identification and expression
- Increase awareness and expression of heartfelt feelings in relation to the key attachment figures in the child's life

Materials
- The Heartfelt Feelings Coloring Card Strategies (HFCCS) Kit that includes a Clinical Manual and 20 expressive and 20 relational cards. The kit can be ordered from the Coloring Card Company (www.coloringcardcompany.com) or by calling (908) 237–2500. Additional sets of cards can be ordered as needed.
- Crayons, markers, or colored pencils for the child to color the heart, and pencils or pens for the child to write in the card

Description
The Heartfelt Feelings Coloring Card Strategies (HFCCS) Kit is a series of strategies that use the potent symbol of the heart shape in therapeutic activities. The strategies are inviting and natural to children (coloring and writing in greeting cards) and can be used in play therapy, child therapy, family therapy, group therapy, and art therapy to facilitate the expression and sharing of heartfelt emotions (Crenshaw, 2007, 2008).

The greeting cards were developed in collaboration with the Coloring Card Company, which makes greeting cards for children created by child artists. The HFCCS has the unique feature of emphasizing two core domains: the expressive and the relational. In the expressive domain the child is instructed to pick a feeling from a group of 40 emotions in the Clinical Manual. The feelings are arranged from simple such as "sad" to more complex such as "perplexed" — the latter would be appropriate for children at the upper limit of the age range.

The child is then directed to pick a color to go with the feeling. If the child picks blue for sad, for example, she/he will then be asked to color in the heart on the front of the greeting card with the color blue. When finished, the child is instructed to write about a time when her/his heart was filled with sadness on the inside of the card on the lines provided. This gives the child an opportunity to express the heartfelt feeling in the context that produced the feeling. If the child is too young to write, she/he can dictate the response and the practitioner can write it on the inside of the card.

In the relational domain the clinical manual contains specific directives for the child that allows for exploration of their social world, for example, "Draw in the heart on the front of the card a person who once was in your heart but no longer is." The relational component consists of systematic exploration of the heartfelt feelings in connection with key attachment figures and with important persons in the child's interpersonal world. The relational cards have the heart shape on the front of the card but the instructions on the inside of the card are different from the expressive cards. Using the example above, the child would be asked on the inside panel of the card to write or dictate a note to the person who was once in her/his heart but no longer is.

Discussion
Many practitioners have used some variation of the heart shape in child, play, art therapy and other creative arts therapies. The expressive domain offers structured therapeutic practice in identifying, labeling, and expressing feelings. These are key skills in affect regulation and for developing social competence. Allan Schore (2003), in his groundbreaking work on affect regulation, has demonstrated that affect dysregulation is central to almost all forms of psychopathology. Therapeutic interventions that address this crucial deficit will have wide application across the psychodiagnostic spectrum.

The relational domain emphasizes that our most heartfelt emotions do not develop in a vacuum. They develop in an interpersonal context. The social context is critical. Some children get angry at school but not at home. The main value of this therapeutic activity is that it creates an entry point for the child to further explore her/his heartfelt feelings and the interpersonal context that elicits them.

The Clinical Manual also contains a number of variations of the HFCCS for use in bereavement work, supervision, examining countertransference feelings, and highlighting strengths in the child, group, or family therapy.

References
Crenshaw, D.A. (2007). *The heartfelt feelings coloring card strategies (HFCCS).* Rhinebeck, NY: Rhinebeck Child and Family Publications.

Crenshaw, D.A. (2008). *Therapeutic engagement of children and adolescents: Play, symbol, drawing, and storytelling strategies.* Lanham, MD: Jason Aronson/Rowman and Littlefield.

Schore, A.N. (2003a). *Affect dysregulation and disorders of the self.* New York: Norton.

About The Author
David A. Crenshaw, Ph.D., ABPP, is a Board Certified Clinical Psychologist by the American Board of Professional Psychology and a Registered Play Therapist Supervisor by the Association for Play Therapy. He is the author of *Therapeutic Engagement of Children and Adolescents: Play, Symbol, Drawing and Storytelling Strategies; Evocative Strategies in Child and Adolescent Psychotherapy;* and co-author with John B. Mordock of the *Handbook of Play Therapy with Aggressive Children and Understanding the Aggression of Children: Fawns in Gorilla Suits.* He is the editor of a new book: *Child and Adolescent Psychotherapy: Wounded Spirits and Healing Paths.*

Draw-A-Story
Source: Jennifer Mariaschin

Theme: Feelings Expression
Recommended Age Range: Seven to Twelve
Treatment Modality: Individual

Goals
- Increase the child's comfort with communicating feelings
- Increase the child's comfort with art as a modality for therapy
- Increase the child's ability to work collaboratively and take turns

Materials
- Blank paper
- Markers, crayons, or colored pencils

Description
This technique allows for the practitioner and the client to collaborate on telling a story. The practitioner starts by asking the client to draw a picture of anything she/he likes. If the client does not want to draw the picture, the practitioner offers to start. The practitioner may start with something very neutral and narrate starting with "once upon a time." For example, if the practitioner draws a picture of a sun, she/he may say, "Once upon a time, there was a sunny day." If the practitioner draws a stick figure and the client is a boy, the practitioner may write, "Once upon a time, there was a boy."

The practitioner then invites the client to add to the picture. The client may interpret this as drawing another picture next to the practitioner's first picture, or the client may add on to the existing picture. The practitioner encourages the client to add her/his part of the story. The practitioner and the client take turns until the story is completed. At each turn, the client and practitioner have to start from the beginning to remember what part of the story was added with the addition of each new picture.

After one full run that allows the client to get used to the activity, the practitioner may then add to the activity by touching on themes that are relevant to therapy. For example, the practitioner may say, "And suddenly it began to rain, so the person/ animal/object (the subject of the story) became angry," and then guide the client through developing an appropriate reaction.

Discussion
Children are reluctant to engage in creative activities because of feelings of anxiety or lack of practice. This technique is useful because it allows children to tell stories in a safe and structured setting, with active support from the practitioner. Children can

build their capacity to tell their own stories and practitioners can guide the theme of the activity to suit their needs, helping children to work collaboratively. This method can also be adapted to groups.

About The Author
Jennifer Mariaschin, LMSW, received her Bachelor's degree at Wesleyan University in 2005 as a psychology major. Jennifer received her MSW from NYU School of Social Work in 2007. She currently works as a mental health clinician at the Institute for Family Health River Center for Counseling in the Bronx, New York.

Memory Quilt or Pillow
Source: Theresa Fraser

Theme: Feelings Expression
Recommended Age Range: Six and Up
Treatment Modality: Individual

(Note: Allow at least five sessions with the client, then one session for the client to share the quilt or pillow with his/her current caregiver.)

Goals
- Gather information about the client's interests, feelings, and needs
- Increase open communication
- Allow the client to discuss positive experiences shared with significant caregivers
- Encourage the client to identify and verbally express the loss of significant past relationships with natural family members or with foster families
- Help the client to identify goals for current or future relationships

Materials
- Photographs – these can come from the child, other adults, or the practitioner. If there are no photographs available, the practitioner may need to research aspects of the child's life by going "online" and, for example, getting pictures of the hospital where the client was born or of an elementary school she/he attended; finding a cultural symbol that represents the client's heritage or symbol of a town that the client has lived in (if there are available sessions, this research can be completed with the client)
- Pieces of clothing that belong to the client and/or to special people in the client's life that will be cut into swatches
- Iron-on transfer paper or photocopy transfer paper that is available at specialty craft stores and office supply stores
- Iron and ironing board
- Sewing machine
- Single flat sheet that has been pre-washed
- White broadcloth that can be used to heat-press photocopies of the gathered photographs as well as to "square up" the clothing pieces into the correct shape of the flat sheet
- Single quilt batting
- Thread for sewing the material swatches together and then quilt thread or wool to attach the three layers of material
- Sewing needles with an eye big enough to accommodate thread or wool
- Sewing scissors
- Camera to take pictures of the work as it is completed from session to session for the client's memory book and the clinical file

Advance Preparation

Contact special people in the client's life to request her/his old clothing for the memory quilt. If the client does not have photos of identified individuals, ask other significant adults in the client's life, such as a Child Protection Worker, to gather photographs.

Explain the purpose of the activity to the client's current caregivers. It is likely that the client will be reminded of past relationships and or experiences and may need additional support from the caregivers if a session's content causes an emotion or memory to be triggered.

Note: It is extremely important to have an accurate social history of the client. For example, it would not be therapeutic to include the photograph of a past perpetrator on the client's quilt or pillow.

Description

The client makes a list of important and positive relationships that she/he has experienced. These can be both current and past relationships.

Once the clothing is gathered (see advance preparation), the client decides which part of the jeans, for example, she/he would like to include in the quilt or pillow. Cut these pieces of clothing into swatches.

Photocopy the photographs onto the iron-on paper. Photos can be enlarged if the client does not have many to work with. The practitioner could also give the client a disposable camera that she/he can use to take pictures of special places and people in her/his current life.

Using the iron, press the iron-on paper with the photographs onto the white broadcloth.

Sew clothing swatches together, trying to use the single sheet as the template.

When the pieces have created the top layer, flip the layer over to face the good side of the single flat sheet. Then place the quilt batting underneath both of these layers. Attach all three layers by sewing pins with the sharp points facing outwards. Place the material on the sewing machine, start at the edge of a long side and sew all three layers together, stopping at the bottom of the quilt. Sew all three edges again so the three layers are held together with two rows of thread. Remove the pins.

Turn the layers inside out so the batting is the middle of the quilt "sandwich" and the clothing layer and flat sheet layer are the top and the bottom. Then fold the edges of the unsewn layer inward and pin the last opening closed with sewing pins.

Sew this end of the quilt closed.

Then with wool or quilting thread at different parts of the quilt, place thread from the top layer down to the bottom layer and then up again. Cut thread/wool and then tie in a knot, cut more thread/wool and tie in a knot. Repeat this action at least six inches in another direction.

Listening to the client during each session is important in order to ascertain how to process the activity with the client once the quilt is completed. The client may verbalize unresolved life/relationship themes that become the roadmap for the processing part of this treatment intervention. Some questions that may be valuable in order to assist the client to connect the activities with feelings activated and experiences revisited include:

- When you close your eyes and feel or smell the quilt, what comes to mind?
- If _____ was here to see your creation, how would you introduce it to him/her?
- What was the most happy, sad, or angry experience that you thought about while we made this quilt?
- Were you reminded of any experience that you haven't thought of for a while?
- Has this activity made you want to begin any other projects or tasks?

Discussion

This activity is not only time consuming but it can also trigger memories for the client. That is why gathering an accurate social history and involving other members of the client's treatment team are important. In this way, the client will receive necessary support between activity sessions.

I have successfully completed this therapeutic process with three clients. It provided one of my adolescent clients with the opportunity to process the positive relationships that he had created in a group-home setting, which he was leaving. The quilt became his termination activity. In addition, he created a second quilt for the group-home staff and wrote some of his own poetry onto the quilt pieces that expressed how he felt about the difference they had made in his life.

In another instance, the group-home staff was struggling with a pre-teen who did not want to wear newly purchased clothing that actually fit him. He could not let go of his now too-small wardrobe, and my suspicion was validated (when it became apparent while making his quilt) that this was because of the memories he had attached to the clothing given to him by previous caregivers. As we began to make the quilt, he began to discuss both the positive and negative past memories and experiences attached to the clothing, memories that included caregiver rejection.

He then was able to use the finished product as a way to symbolize his resiliency and his ability to look at how previous experiences had helped him to become the person he was today.

During our sessions, he was triggered by the clothing items themselves, but he also began to be aware of his reaction to these sensory triggers. For example, one T-shirt smelled like an old foster parent, another sweatshirt made him feel safe when he touched it repetitively. This new awareness helped him to develop a self-care plan when feeling anxious in stressful situations. At these times, he could "wrap" himself in the quilt and feel the love he had once received from others.

For clients who have experienced rejection and abuse, the quilt can become a way to process past successes and losses. However, since this activity may trigger strong emotions or memories, it is helpful to provide "grounding" and/or predictable activities for each session, such as non-directive play time or playing a specific game each week.

About The Author

Theresa Fraser, C.C.W., B.A., has worked in the mental health field for the last 25 years and currently utilizes the play therapy process with children, teens and families. She has a diploma in General Social Work, Certificate in Child Abuse Prevention, and she is a Trauma and Loss Clinical Specialist. She has also completed the Canadian Association for Child and Play Therapy Certificate Program and has received extensive training in Sandtray/Worldplay. She teaches part time in the Child and Youth Worker program at Humber College. She and her husband Kevin have fostered over 200 children/adolescents.

Making Tear Soup
Source: Sally A. Loughrin

Theme: Feelings Expression (Grief)
Recommended Age Range: Eight to Thirteen
Treatment Modality: Individual, Group, Family

Goals
- Increase awareness of normal feelings of grief
- Verbally identify and express feelings

Materials
- A copy of *Tear Soup: A Recipe for Healing after Loss* by Pat Schwiebert and Chick DeKlyen (Portland, Oregon: Grief Watch, 2005)
- Plastic containers with covers, one for each child
- Pens
- Markers
- Pencils
- Pieces of paper or 3" x 5" index cards

Description
The practitioner reads the book *Tear Soup: A Recipe for Healing after Loss* and briefly discusses it with the client. Process questions might include:

- Why was Grandy making tear soup?
- What was the purpose of her tear soup?
- What did Grandy mean when she said that "grief is never clean"?
- How did the people in Grandy's life try to help her feel better? Were they successful?

The practitioner tells the client, "You are going to be a cook today and you will be making tear soup." The client is provided with a soup pot and cover (plastic container with cover) and writes TEAR SOUP on each of the four sides. Then, on the paper or index cards, the client writes down the ingredients for her/his own tear soup. If the client is having difficulty thinking of ingredients, ask her/him to name some of the ingredients that Grandy put into her tear soup.

When finished, ask the client to share the ingredients she/he put into the soup. Also, discuss what was learned from the book and from making her/his own tear soup.

Discussion
Children and teenagers need to hear that all of their feelings are normal and okay and that feelings are not right/wrong or good/bad, they do not have to be explained or defended, they just are. It is important to emphasize that feelings be

expressed in ways that do not hurt the person (with the feelings), another person, or a thing. This tear soup exercise helps clients recognize that all grieving people experience a myriad of uncomfortable feelings, and it gives them some healthy ways of expressing those feelings.

About The Author

Sally A. Loughrin, LMSW, MA, is a licensed social worker and is completing the requirements to become a certified play therapist. She works as a bereavement social worker with children and teenagers at Angela Hospice in Livonia, Michigan. She has written the following articles that were published in *Bereavement Magazine:* "Books as a Resource for Children," "Story Writing: A Technique," and "The Kids Need to Know."

Family and Personal Changes Game
Source: Sally A. Loughrin

Theme: Feelings Expression (Grief)
Recommended Age Range: Nine to Adult
Treatment Modality: Individual, Group, Family

Goals
- Increase the understanding that there are many changes after the death of a loved one
- Help normalize the fact that the changes occur

Materials
- JENGA™ Game
- Family and Personal Changes Game Questions (included)

Advance Preparation
With a fine-tipped marker, write the numbers 1 through 27 on 27 of the JENGA blocks. Set up the block tower making certain that the blocks with the numbers on them are facing down.

Description
The object of the game is to remove as many of the blocks without toppling the tower.

As each player removes a block, ask her/him to see if there is a number on the bottom. If the block is blank, the next client takes a turn. If there is a number on the bottom, the client will read the corresponding question from the list of "Family and Personal Changes Game Questions" (see below) and respond. If the client is unable to respond, ask if anyone else can provide an answer. The game continues in this manner until the tower falls. Once this happens, ask the clients to respond to the questions for the numbers on the remaining blocks.

Discussion
Many different types of changes tend to be imposed on children and teens who have experienced the death of someone they love. While some of the changes may be positive and comfortable, most of them are less positive and uncomfortable. Often, such changes are easier to accept if the children and teens understand that these changes are normal and that many of their peers have experienced similar changes.

The questions or statements in the game provide a basis for further discussion. Possible process questions might include:

1) In thinking about all of the changes in your life since the death, what do you think has been the most important one?

2) ____ said she always took it for granted that her ____ would always be here, and now she realizes how special the important people in her life are. Have any of the rest of you had similar thoughts?

3) _____ said he thought he was not accepting the fact that he has to do more chores at home since ____ died. What do the rest of you think about this?

4) Did you find it interesting that ____ said the people she thought were her friends seemed to abandon her after the death, and people she barely knew have become her close friends? Have any of the rest of you had a similar experience with friendships?

The game can be adapted for other client populations.

About The Author

Sally A. Loughrin, LMSW, MA, is a licensed social worker and is completing the requirements to become a certified play therapist. She works as a bereavement social worker with children and teenagers at Angela Hospice in Livonia, Michigan. She has written the following articles that were published in *Bereavement Magazine:* "Books as a Resource for Children," "Story Writing: A Technique," and "The Kids Need to Know."

Family and Personal Changes Game
Questions

1. Explain how the death has changed you.

2. List one change in your home since the death that has been difficult for you to accept? Explain the reason.

3. Name two changes since the death that you do not like.

4. How has the death of your loved one changed the way you think about death?

5. How has the way you celebrate holidays changed since your loved one died? Explain.

6. What do you think it means when you hear that when there is a death of someone you love, there are always losses and changes?

7. Think about all of the changes that have occurred since the death and list one good change.

8. Have you changed the way you would talk to another child who lost a loved one as you did? Explain.

9. Complete this statement: "I think I would feel better if only I could change _____."

10. Name two changes in your family since the death that have bothered you the most. Explain.

11. List one family tradition that has changed since the death.

12. Name two feelings you have had about the changes in your life since the death.

13. What do you think is the hardest part of any kind of change? Explain.

14. How has the death changed the way you think about your own life? Explain.

15. In what way has the death changed the way you live your life?

16. What family members have changed the most since the death? Do you know why?

17. How have your friendships changed since the death? Explain.

18. Have your responsibilities at home changed since the death? If so, how?

19. List one way you would have changed this year even if the death had not happened. Explain.

20. What family tradition has stayed the same since the death?

21. What do you think might be a change that will take place in your family in the next year?

22. How has your attitude about what is important in life changed since the death?

23. In what way has your everyday routine changed since the death? Explain.

24. Complete this sentence: "The biggest loss or change other than the death of my loved one has been _____." Explain your answer.

25. How have the changes in your life seemed different from the ones in your other family members?

26. What have you done that has helped you the most with all of the changes in your life since the death? Explain.

27. What changes have you had in school in the past year?

If Grief Was a Color
Source: Kathryn A. Markell and Marc A. Markell

Theme: Feelings Expression (Grief)
Recommended Age Range: Twelve to Sixteen
Treatment Modality: Individual, Group

Goals
- Verbally identify and express feelings
- Increase open communication
- Gather information about the client's feelings and needs

Materials
- Paper
- Pen
- Activity Sheet (included)

Advance Preparation
Photocopy the Activity Sheet.

Description
The client completes the Activity Sheet and then discusses her/his responses. Process questions include:

(1) Which responses were easiest/most difficult for you to think of? Why?

(2) Reflect on whether all of your responses were negative. Why? If no, which were positive images and why where they positive?

(3) Discuss images of grief and death you have heard in poems, songs, or stories.

(4) Discuss any poems, songs, or stories that help you to feel better when you think about the person who has died. Why?

If in a group, have the clients discuss any similar responses they gave and why those same terms came to mind.

As an extension to the activity, the client can select one of the lines from the Activity Sheet as the starting line to write a poem or song.

Discussion
Adolescents are just beginning to think abstractly. This often leads them to obsess

about abstract concepts, like "the meaning of life" and "what happens after you die." These are fascinating issues that have no correct answer, and so they provide infinite ground for speculation. Adolescents who are grieving may be especially at risk for "over-obsession" about topics related to death and dying. It may help them to verbalize their views about grief and death by having them complete this activity where they are asked to picture grief and death in a variety of creative ways.

Reference
Markell, Kathryn A., and Marc A. Markell. (2008). *The children who lived: Using Harry Potter and other fictional characters to help grieving children and adolescents.* New York: Routledge.

About The Authors
Kathryn A. Markell, Ph.D., teaches child and adolescent psychology at Anoka-Ramsey Community College in Coon Rapids, Minnesota, and researches and writes in the area of grief and loss.

Marc A. Markell, Ph.D., CT, is a professor at St. Cloud State University in St. Cloud, Minnesota. He teaches courses, presents workshops, facilitates grief groups, and researches and writes in the area of grief and loss.

If Grief Was a Color
Activity Sheet

If death was a color it would be _____.

If death was an animal it would be _____.

If death was a song it would be _____.

If death was a flavor it would be _____.

If death was a season it would be _____.

If death was a sound it would be _____.

If death was a building it would be _____.

If grief was a color it would be _____.

If grief was an animal it would be _____.

If grief was a song it would be _____.

If grief was a flavor it would be _____.

If grief was a season it would be _____.

If grief was a sound it would be _____.

If grief was a building it would be _____.

© Kathryn A. Markell and Marc A. Markell

96

Your Heart
Source: Sally A. Loughrin

Theme: Feelings Expression (Grief)
Recommended Age Range: Eight to Adult
Treatment Modality: Individual, Group, Family

Goals
- To increase the client's understanding of the meaning of grief
- To create a visual that symbolizes one's individual grief

Materials
- A heart shape that is made from a sheet of thin foam, cut into pieces (one for each person)
- A heart shape that is made from foam that remains in one piece
- Plastic bags (one for each person)
- White cardstock (one piece for each person)
- Glue sticks (one for each person)
- One uncut heart glued to a piece of white cardstock

Advance Preparation
Cut the hearts into pieces and place them into the plastic bags (one for each person). The hearts should be cut into four to seven pieces for younger children and multiple smaller pieces for older children and teens.

Description
The practitioner gives the client a plastic bag and tells the client that the bag contains pieces that look like a puzzle. When the pieces are put together, they will form a heart.

The client is asked to put the puzzle together on the piece of white cardstock. When the heart is formed, the client is given a glue stick and glues the heart pieces to the cardstock.

When the client's heart is glued onto the cardstock, the practitioner asks the client to compare her/his foam heart with the uncut sample foam heart. The practitioner indicates that when there is a death of someone special, it is like having a heart that is broken. The following points are then highlighted:

- While it is possible to put one's broken heart back together with the glue stick, it is not exactly the same as it was before the death. There are marks where the pieces were glued.
- Those marks are like the scars on one's heart when a person has

97

experienced the death of a loved one.

- The glued or repaired heart can be as strong as the unbroken one, but it is still not quite the same.
- The glued together heart can be compared with people who are never quite the same after a death.
- The new "you" can be as strong as the "you" before the death, but you will be different and will always have the scars caused from the death.
- In time, the scars will actually help you think of all the good memories you had with the special person who died.

Discussion

Children and teens who have experienced the death of someone they love have uncomfortable feelings but often do not understand what those feelings are and why they are there. It is helpful to let them know that the death of a loved one changes those surviving forever. With this activity, it is possible to help the client understand that it is natural to grieve, to cry, to have many uncomfortable feelings, and it is also possible to reach a level of acceptance that is needed in order to move forward.

<u>About The Author</u>

Sally A. Loughrin, LMSW, MA, is a licensed social worker and is completing the requirements to become a certified Play therapist. She works as a bereavement social worker with children and teenagers at Angela Hospice in Livonia, Michigan. She has written the following articles that were published in *Bereavement Magazine:* "Books as a Resource for Children," "Story Writing: A Technique," and "The Kids Need to Know."

© Sally A. Loughrin

Circles of Support
Source: Denise O'Neill

Theme: Feelings Expression (Grief)
Recommended Age Range: Four to Seven
Treatment Modality: Individual

Goals
- Increase feelings vocabulary
- Increase awareness regarding how feelings change
- Gather information about the client's support network

Materials
- Lasagna-size pan
- Milk
- Food coloring: blue, red, yellow
- Q-tip or eye dropper
- Dish liquid detergent

Description
The practitioner pours enough milk in the lasagna-size pan to completely cover the bottom and allows it to settle. The practitioner states, "When someone we love dies, we have many different feelings. We may wish some of these feelings would go away. These new feelings can be scary. Grown-ups call these feelings grief."

The practitioner invites the child to name some of the feelings we know. The three key feelings that are identified are sad, angry, and happy. The practitioner explains that each of the food colors represents one of the identified feelings. As the practitioner states the feeling associated with a specific color, the practitioner adds one drop of that particular food coloring to the milk. (Each drop will form a separate circle of color.)

The blue food coloring represents sad.

The red food coloring represents angry.

The yellow food coloring represents happy.

The child is then asked to think about a time when she/he felt sad. The practitioner asks the child to name someone who is there when she/he feels sad. While the child names a person, invite the child to take the Q-tip dipped in dish liquid and to touch the centre of the blue circle. Next, ask the child to think about a time when she/he felt angry. The practitioner asks the child to name someone who is there when she/he feels angry. While the child names a person, invite the child to take the Q-tip dipped in dish liquid and to touch the centre of the red circle. Next, ask the child to think about a time when she/he felt happy. While the child names a person, invite the child to take the Q-tip dipped in dish liquid and to touch the centre of the yellow circle.

The practitioner engages the child in a discussion to name family and friends who care about her/him and who have helped her/him. The practitioner offers the child reassurance that all feelings are okay and that it helps to have someone to listen, to love. Watch as the individual circles erupt and expand to form a rainbow of color. The practitioner states, "This is your Circle of Support. Watch the Circle of Love grow!"

Discussion

The awareness and identification of feelings is the first step in the child's grief process. When someone is grieving, it can be hard to find comfort. It helps to have someone to listen, to love. The child becomes a witness to the magic of having many people love and care about them. The practitioner can extend this activity to include a discussion on how our feelings do change.

Note: This activity can be modified to other populations, including a child who is presenting with signs of depression. It can help the child increase awareness of various feelings states, develop awareness that feelings do change, and identify people who are supportive.

About The Author

Denise O'Neill, ECE.C, Grief and Bereavement Studies, provides grief support and education for children and adults. She is the creator of PATCH (Parents and Their Children Healing), an interactive grief support program for young children (ages 2 ½ to 7 years) and their families.

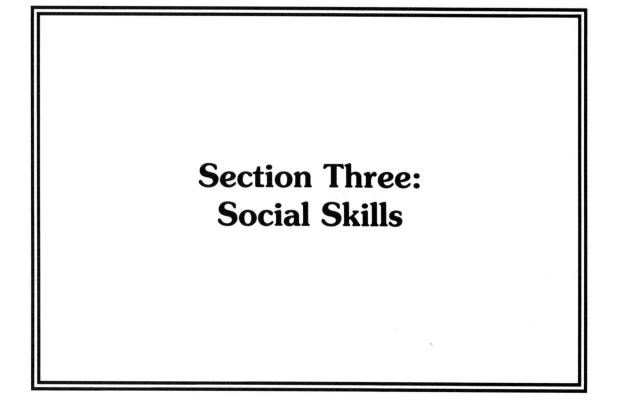

Section Three:
Social Skills

Who's Got the Turtle? Game

Source: Lorie Walton

Theme: Social Skills
Recommended Age Range: Three to Seven
Treatment Modality: Family, Group

Goals
- Increase language skills
- Become more comfortable in approaching others to communicate
- Promote pro-social behaviour such as eye contact, question-asking, turn-taking
- Increase family and/or group cohesion through fun and co-operation

Materials
- Small stuffed turtle (or other small object that can be held in a child's hand)
- Small blanket

Description
Group members sit in a circle facing each other. One child volunteers to go into the center of the circle and the practitioner covers her/him with a blanket (like a turtle shell). Make sure when covering the child with the blanket to ask, "Are you okay under the blanket?" If the child is not okay, then the blanket is removed and the child covers her/his eyes so she/he cannot peek out.

The practitioner begins singing the words to "Who's Got the Turtle?" and passes the turtle to the next person. The turtle continues to be passed around until the song is finished. The last person to have the turtle when the song ends, hides the turtle behind her/his back and then puts her/his hands in front like everyone else, pretending to look like everyone else. The practitioner takes the blanket off of the child in the center. The child then goes around to each person, makes eye contact and asks them by name, such as, "Lorie, do you have the turtle?" The person being asked must answer truthfully, "No, Timmy, I don't have the turtle." The child continues to ask around the circle until the turtle is found. The person who has the turtle must answer honestly, "Yes, Timmy, I have the turtle" and brings the turtle out from behind her/his back. The person who was hiding the turtle now gets to be the person in the middle, covered under the turtle shell (blanket), and the game begins again.

Each person should have a turn in the middle and should have a turn at hiding the turtle. The turtle can be replaced with any other small object (pom-pom, cotton ball, small stuffed bunny, etc.) and, if replaced, the wording of the song can indicate the object being used (e.g., "Who has the pom-pom?").

"Who's Got the Turtle?"
(sung to the tune of "Pop Goes the Weasel")

Round and round the turtle goes,
Pass it to your neighbor.
Where it stops nobody knows.
Who's got the turtle?

Discussion

Young children and families enjoy this game. Although this game is simple, children take great delight in not only hiding under the blanket but also seeing their parents or friends hiding under the blanket, too. The game develops language and communication skills and helps to develop comfort in social interactions.

It is important for the practitioner to keep the game structured and to remain in control of the game, that is, to be the one to put on the blanket and take it off, pace the song appropriately to the children's ability, use simple language and questions if the children are still developing language and questioning skills.

The practitioner should allow for differences in the group and accommodate the game accordingly. For example, the child who is just learning to speak can ask the question in a one-word format "Turtle?" while the older children or family members can ask at their level of ability. As well, some children (or adults) might try to "tease" by saying they don't have the turtle when they do. The practitioner should not be afraid to stick to the "rules of the game," and can do so by stating, "Remember, in this game we give the truthful answer. If you have the turtle you must show it right away." Many young children as well as children who have experienced trauma or attachment disruptions do not accept "teasing" as pleasurable but rather take it as a rejection. Thus, it is important to keep to the rules by using "honest" answers. This will also keep the flow of the game going smoothly.

About The Author

Lorie Walton, MEd, CPT-S, is a Certified Theraplay® Therapist Trainer Supervisor and the owner and Lead Therapist of Family First Play Therapy Centre Inc., in Bradford, Ontario, a center focused on assisting children and families dealing with attachment, trauma, and emotional issues. In conjunction with her private practice, Lorie is a consultant and Play Therapy Clinical Supervisor for agencies within Ontario and is currently the president of the Canadian Association for Child and Play Therapy (CACPT). She offers workshops on Theraplay®, Attachment and Play Therapy related topics, internship opportunities and supervision to those studying to become certified in Play Therapy and Theraplay®.

Magic Carpet Ride

Source: Liana Lowenstein

Theme: Social Skills
Recommended Age Range: Three to Seven
Treatment Modality: Group

Goals
- Increase socially appropriate behavior with peers
- Participate in peer group activities in a cooperative manner

Materials
- Small carpet or towel large enough for all group members to sit on
- Stickers
- Crayons
- Large piece of paper
- Puzzle
- Jar of bubbles
- Plastic tea set
- Juice and cookies

Description
The group leader enthusiastically tells the children they are going on a magic carpet ride! The leader states that this is a very special journey, and that they will be making four stops. Tell the children that at each stop, there is a task they need to complete. Once the task is completed, they will get a sticker.

Everyone in the group sits on the carpet before setting off on their journey. (The leader should be theatrical and make various comments to help the children make believe they are truly going on a magic carpet ride!)

At the first stop, "The Land of Sharing," the children must color a picture, using the crayons and paper provided. The children must share the crayons, making sure that each group member gets to use each of the crayons for their picture. Once the task is completed, the leader gives each child a sticker. The group then piles onto the magic carpet, and they set off again.

The second stop is "The Land of Waiting Your Turn." Here, the leader passes the bubbles around the group and each child has a turn to blow bubbles. Once all the children have demonstrated the ability to wait their turn for the bubbles, they get another sticker.

The group sits on the carpet again, and they set off for the third stop, "The Land of Working Together." Here the group must work cooperatively to put the puzzle together. If the group is not working cooperatively, the leader takes the puzzle apart, and has them start over again. The leader can offer suggestions to facilitate group cooperation. Once the puzzle is completed, the leader gives each child another sticker.

The group then travels to the final destination, "The Land of Being Polite." The group has a tea party using the plastic tea set, juice, and cookies. The leader tells the children they must politely say, "Hello, how are you?" "Please pass the cookies," and "Thank you for the tea." Once the tea party is over, the leader gives each child their last sticker, and the group makes its return journey.

Once the children are "home," the group discusses what was learned at each stop on the magic carpet ride.

Discussion
This activity uses imaginative play to help young children strengthen their interpersonal skills. Children will enjoy the magic carpet ride and the journey to the various "lands." Awarding stickers for appropriate social interaction reinforces their positive behavior. The practitioner can make this activity more appealing by incorporating props, costumes, and music for the magic carpet ride.

Reference
Lowenstein, L. (1999). *Creative interventions for troubled children and youth.* Toronto, ON: Champion Press.

About The Author
Liana Lowenstein, MSW, RSW, CPT-S, is a social worker and Certified Play Therapy Supervisor in Toronto. She maintains a private practice, provides clinical supervision and consultation to mental health professionals, and lectures internationally on child and play therapy. She has authored numerous publications, including the books *Paper Dolls and Paper Airplanes: Therapeutic Exercises for Sexually Traumatized Children, Creative Interventions for Troubled Children and Youth, More Creative Interventions for Troubled Children and Youth, Creative Interventions for Bereaved Children,* and *Creative Interventions for Children of Divorce.*

The "Excuse Me" Game
Source: Brenda L. Bierdeman

Theme: Social Skills
Recommended Age Range: Five and Up
Treatment Modality: Individual, Group, Family

Goals
- Increase knowledge of manners and socially appropriate behavior for common hygiene issues
- Practice good manners of saying "Excuse me"
- Increase the likelihood that participants will perform socially appropriate behaviors in real situations of daily life

Materials
- One self-inflating Whoopie Cushion for each participant
- Hygiene questions written or typed onto slips of paper
- Bag or container for questions

Advance Preparation
Make a set of hygiene and manners questions by typing out a list of questions, printing them out, cutting the questions into strips, and placing them in a bag or container.

Description
The practitioner introduces the game as follows: "We're going to play a game to help us learn more about good manners and proper hygiene. Hygiene is what we do to keep our bodies clean and healthy. I'm going to first give each of you a Whoopie Cushion. I will be the reader or we can take turns reading and answering questions. I will read a question and when you think you have the answer, I want you to sit on your cushion and say, 'Excuse me.' The first one to say 'Excuse me' gets to answer the question. We'll keep taking turns until we have answered all the questions."

Discussion
Many participants have difficulty with manners and with hygiene. This game combines the two issues into one and allows the practitioner to address these issues in a very playful, practical, multisensory way. Questions can be tailored to a specific child or family, but in general, the questions can be like the following:
- How often should a person brush their teeth?
- How can you tell if a person needs to wash their hair?
- What should you do if you are eating a meal with your family and you feel like you are going to pass gas?

It is best to keep the questions as short and to the point as possible.

The self-inflating Whoopie Cushions are inexpensive (under $5 each) and allows the game to be fast paced without having to stop and blow the cushions up after each question. For a slower paced game, use regular Whoopie Cushions (under $1 each) and have the participants re-inflate their cushion after each answer. The sound also mimics someone passing gas and connects making the sound with the proper behavior, which is to say "Excuse me." The questions can be made up ahead of time and stored for use with other participants again and again.

The game is the most effective when the practitioner is flexible and changes the parameters as needed. For example, if the clients begin to tire of the game, it can be ended before completing all the questions. If a minimal or even incorrect answer is given, a second question can be asked, such as, "What else might you say?" or "Can anyone else think of an answer?" Following up an answer by saying "Tell me more about that" also encourages participants to elaborate on why they think that is true or helps the practitioner understand more about family rules and traditions or expectations.

Consider taking turns reading the questions to facilitate appropriate behavior or manners. Allowing family or group members to make up their own questions for the game also helps diagnostically to see what the family is concerned about.

About The Author
Brenda L. Bierdeman, Psy.D., CPT-P, is a New York State Licensed Clinical Psychologist, an IBECPT Certified Play Therapist Professor, and member of the Association for Play Therapy. She brings over twenty-five years of experience to her practice of diagnosing and treating children, adolescents, and adults. She has lectured on diagnostic and therapeutic play techniques in the US, Canada, and Central America.

The "May I ... Thank You" Card Game
Source: Norma Leben

Theme: Social Skills
Recommended Age Range: Eight and Up
Treatment Modality: Group, Family

Goals
- Learn and practice pro-social behavior such as good manners, paying attention, and following the rules
- Build trust amongst players
- Lengthen attention span

Materials
- One deck of standard playing cards
- Small prizes (optional)

Advance Preparation
For younger players, modify the game by taking away the face cards (J, Q, K), thus making it easier for their littler hands and ensuring a shorter and less frustrating game.

Description
The game is explained as follows:

"We're going to play a game that's going to help us practice a very important social skill – good manners! It's called the "May I ... Thank You" Card Game. I'm going to begin by distributing all of these cards equally amongst all of the players. The object of the game is to collect 'four-of-a-kind' and each of the four-card set is worth one point. The total number of points from all the cards is 13 points (or 10 if the face cards are taken out).

Now, let's look at all the cards in your hands and group them by their suits, which are Hearts, Diamonds, Clubs, and Spades. In that way, it will be easy for you to locate a card when other players ask for it. (Allow a minute for players to organize their cards. Little hands may need help to fan out their cards.)

To ask for a card, a player will call the name of another player, followed by "May I ..." So, if I want a card from John, I'd say, "John, may I have the two of Hearts please?" If John has the two of Hearts, he will be honest, pick out that card and hand it to me. I MUST say "Thank You" before I touch the card he offers. If I forget to say "Thank You" and grab the card, John keeps that card, then he takes his turn to ask others for cards.

108

If John does not have the two of Hearts, he will reply, "Sorry, I do not have that card," Then John takes his turn to ask others for cards.

If I use good manners and obtain a card from another player, I can continue to ask others for cards until I'm turned down by another player. Once a player has collected 'four-of-a-kind,' she/he places that stack of cards down on the table and earns a point. The game ends when all 13 (or 10 without face cards) sets of the 'four-of-a-kind' have been collected. The person who gets the most points wins. Are there any questions? If not, let's begin and we'll learn the rules as we play."

Discussion

This game generates a lot of excitement and laughter. The practitioner may be one of the players in order to model social skills such as good manners, paying attention, following the rules, and sportsmanship. Or, the practitioner may team up with the youngest player to even out the playing field. During the game, the practitioner reminds players to be honest in releasing cards, acts as the umpire to watch for ill-mannered players, and reinforces rules of the game. The practitioner also compliments players who exercise good manners and congratulates players who earn points.

Sometimes there are sore losers in a group of players. They panic after a few players collect their "four-of-a-kind" sets. The practitioner can reassure them by saying: "The game has just begun." "There are 13 points to be earned by all." "Let's pay attention and see how others ask for cards." "Well, it's only a game, not the end of the world." "See, I don't get any points yet." "Yes, you've got a good memory, now remember to say thank you more often." However, in spite of all these stop-gap interventions, a sore loser may still become angry and disrupt the game, for example, by tearing up cards and throwing them on the floor. The practitioner should make every attempt to intervene and shift this negative behavior to more pro-social behavior. However, if the child does not respond, the practitioner may have to end the game by calmly stating, "Apparently we're not ready to play this game today. Maybe we'll wait and try again another day!" If this happens, the practitioner calmly collects all the cards and introduces another game, which is why it's advisable to prepare more games than needed.

Sometimes children have difficulty accepting defeat, even in a game situation, and their anger explodes in the form of throwing things, pushing everything off the table, or even overturning the table! These children will need more direct anger-management interventions.

At the end of the game, the practitioner leads a short discussion on why some players earned more points than others. The reasons could be using good manners, paying attention to who does not have the requested cards, memorizing who needs what cards, keeping a positive attitude even while others are earning points first. Small prizes can be set aside, and the player who earns the most points may have the first pick of these token prizes.

When family members play this game, the process quickly reveals the habitual use or absence of manners as well as mutual respect in their home.

Reference
Leben, Norma Y. (1999). *Directive group play therapy: 60 structured games for the treatment of ADHD, low self-esteem, and traumatized children.* Pflugerville, TX. Morning Glory Treatment Center for Children.

About The Author
Norma Leben, MSW, LCSW, ACSW, RPT-S, CPT-P. Since graduating with a University of Chicago MSSA, she has worked as a CPS supervisor, school dropout team leader, residential treatment supervisor, executive director, and international trainer. She is a licensed clinical social worker and Play Therapy Supervisor who has authored over 45 audio or video recordings, books, and publications in English and Chinese on parenting and play therapy techniques.

The Banana Game
Source: Norma Leben

Theme: Social Skills
Recommended Age Range: Nine to Adult
Treatment Modality: Group, Family (3 players)

Goals
- Increase awareness of the components necessary for successful teamwork (an achievable goal, leader and follower roles, and good communication skills)
- Illustrate how good communication requires a complete cycle (giving clear directions, listening, following instructions, and giving constructive feedback)

Materials
- Banana
- 12" dinner plate
- Fork
- Knife

Description
This game requires three players. If the group size is bigger than three, the practitioner will ask for three volunteers and the others will be observers.

Set up the game as follows: A team of three players will be seated on the same side of a table. The person in the middle is called the Brain. He is the only one who is allowed to talk. The Brain's job is to tell the others what to do to get the job done. He keeps both of his arms and hands behind his back so that he cannot touch anything.

The person on the Brain's left is Lefty. She is robot-like and not allowed to talk or ask questions or make assumptions about past experience. She can only use her left arm and hand. Her right arm will be placed on Brain's back. If the instruction given to her is unclear as to what to do, where to do it, and what size is expected, she will not be able to perform any actions.

The person on Brain's right is Righty. She is also robot-like, not allowed to talk, ask questions or make assumptions about past experience. She can only use her right arm and hand. Her left arm will be placed on Brain's back. If the instruction given to her is unclear as to what to do, where to do it, and what size is expected, she will not be able to perform any actions.

The practitioner ensures that all players maintain their postures during the game.

The practitioner places an unpeeled banana on the plate in front of the Brain. On the left side of the plate is a fork and on the right side is a knife.

The practitioner explains the roles of every team member. The practitioner explains that the goal of the game is for them to work together so that the banana is peeled, cut into edible chunks, and all three members of the team are fed one piece.

Afterwards, the practitioner asks the observers and players to share what they saw and asks for their suggestions for a smoother, quicker result. The team members should share their personal experiences and not blame others for problems. The practitioner should encourage self-reflective comments such as these from the Brain:

> I guess I was taking my communication for granted, like when I said, "Righty, take the peel off the banana." Righty didn't do it because it was impossible. Then I had to change and make it more exact, "Lefty, please hold the banana 12 inches in front of me so that Righty can peel it. Hold it still. Now you can lower the banana down on the plate."

As a closing to the activity, the practitioner can ask the members to list what was learned about communication and teamwork.

Discussion

When the game begins, the Brain starts giving instructions and soon finds out that without clear and specific directions his intentions will not be carried out by Lefty or Righty, causing frustration for all parties. The Brain may have to do many self-corrections to help the team members perform their sequential small robot-like movements. The process will also focus on paying attention and listening and following instructions before everyone gets a bite of banana and the game ends.

It is suggested that this game be played more than once and that the players change roles so that each will feel the challenges and problem-solving skills needed in being the Brain, Lefty, and Righty.

This game is also helpful for assessing communication skills and tolerance for frustration. During the game, the practitioner facilitates problem ownership and insight development by letting the team struggle before coaching on giving specific instruction, listening carefully, and following instructions. After the game, the practitioner can remind members that to reduce conflicts in real life, members can encourage questions, ask for clarification, take a few calming breaths, and give credit for helpful suggestions.

About The Author

Norma Leben, MSW, LCSW, ACSW, RPT-S, CPT-P. Since graduating with a University of Chicago MSSA, Norma has worked as a CPS supervisor, school dropout team leader, residential treatment supervisor, executive director, and international trainer. She is a licensed clinical social worker and play therapy supervisor who has authored over 45 audio or video recordings, books, and publications in English and Chinese on parenting and play therapy techniques.

InventoGame
Source: Maria Roberts

Theme: Social Skills
Recommended Age Range: Twelve and Up
Treatment Modality: Group

Goals
- Practice pro-social behavior such as leadership, communication, and following rules
- Participate in a peer group activity in a cooperative manner
- Increase self-esteem through accomplishment and creative process

Materials
- Two ping pong balls or similar objects
- One large piece of cardboard
- String or wire
- 2 Styrofoam cups
- Five coffee stirrers
- One small square piece of cardboard
- Five paperclips
- 20 index cards
- One die
- Markers
- Scissors
- Tape

Description
The group leader discusses the role creative teams play in various companies that are involved in developing games. The group also discusses teams and the development of roles, that is, leaders, observers, cheerleaders, peacekeepers, and so on. The group is then separated into two teams. Each team is asked to develop a game with the materials available. The teams can use as many or as few of the materials as they wish.

Each game will need to have an objective or definition of how to win the game and identify the game's rules, the intended age group, and the number of players.

Both teams have a limit of 30 minutes to develop their game using only the available materials.

Group facilitators or designated group members are assigned as the observers to rate each team in the following areas of the team process: cooperation, efficiency, participation of members, creativity, and usability. Teams are rated on a scale of one to five with one being poor and five being excellent. As an optional incentive, the team with the most points earns a reward.

Once the games have been created, each team presents their game to the rest of the group.

Discussion

Adolescents are preoccupied with finding their identity by experiencing various roles. They are eager to find where they may fit in in a group setting. Their self-esteem can be developed through the creative process and through their contribution to the development of an end product. Each member has the opportunity to contribute to the team activity, developing social skills as they work to earn points for the team. While participating in this activity, adolescents can feel a sense of accomplishment and of having made a contribution, notwithstanding any challenges they may experience. A sense of resilience is developed through this group process.

About The Author

Maria Roberts, LCSW, RPT-S, currently provides therapeutic individual and group counseling at Phillips Programs, a special education setting to all age levels. For many years she has worked as a clinical social worker in the mental health setting in the public and private sectors. She has provided supervision to student interns and other professionals. She currently maintains a private practice in Reston, Virginia, in addition to her work in the school setting. She has implemented play therapy techniques in the United States and abroad in a variety of settings serving children, adolescents, and adults.

Community Building Sand Tray
Source: Barbara Jones Warrick

Treatment Theme: Social Skills
Recommended Age Range: Eight to Adult
Treatment Modality: Group, Family (up to eight participants)

Goals
- Increase group cohesion
- Practice and experience success in taking turns and negotiating

Materials
- Sand tray
- Sand tray objects (representing various categories: people, animals, plants, buildings, vehicles, etc.)

Description
Decide on a topic common to the participants and ask each participant to select up to three sand tray objects. For example, a grief group may be asked to build on the theme of funerals, or a group of teens may be asked to build on the theme of friendship. Invite participants to pay attention to the selection process and to notice how it feels:

- Being limited to three objects
- When someone else takes an object they want
- When they cannot find what they need

Ask each participant to place her/his first object in the tray. Ask them once again to place an object in the tray, this time starting with person number two. Repeat for the third object starting with person number three, and so on. Let participants know they may not move or touch other people's objects.

When the building phase is completed, direct participants to look at the tray from a variety of perspectives — for example, from each side, from above and below. Invite participants to pay attention to the placement process and to notice:

- How it feels to place their objects
- How it feels when the place they want is taken
- How it feels when someone places their object next to/near theirs
- How the tray changes depending on their viewing position
- Their overall reaction to the tray

Starting with person number four, ask each participant to add, subtract, move, or otherwise change the tray in one way. When the changes are completed, direct

116

participants to look at the tray from a variety of perspectives. Invite them to pay attention to the change process and to notice:

- How the tray changes
- How it feels when they move or remove someone else's object
- How it feels when someone else moves or removes their object
- How the tray changes depending on their viewing position
- Their overall reaction to the tray

Starting with person number five, invite each participant to say something about the building experience.

Starting with person number six, invite each participant to say something about the change experience.

Starting with person number seven, invite each participant to give a title or briefly describe the teaching he/she believes this tray has to offer.

Starting with person number eight, invite each participant to select one word from the titles/teachings that have been shared.

Take the words and form them into a short title or sentence that represents the sand tray. This will reflect to the participants the richness of the experiences they have shared.

Discussion

Providing participants with a shared approach to the creation of a sand tray allows them to observe their own processes and reactions as well as those of other participants and experience a stronger sense of connection to others. The structure of this activity gives participants with the successful experience of taking turns building and negotiating.

About The Author

Barbara Jones Warrick, M.Ed., CPT-S, is a graduate of the M.Ed. Counseling program at the University of Western Ontario. She is a child and family therapist working in private practice and agency settings, and she is a Certified Child and Play Therapist supervisor with the Canadian Association for Child and Play Therapy and the International Board of Examiners of Certified Play Therapists. She has completed the training with Gisela Schubach De Domenico in Sand Tray World Play and has also completed training in the Erica Method with Mararetta Sjolund. She teaches sand tray therapy and uses sand tray extensively in her work with children, families, groups, and individuals.

Paint Spots
Source: Kim D. O'Connor

Theme: Social Skills
Recommended Age Range: Eight and Up
Treatment Modality: Individual or Group

Goals
- Help client recognize and think about how others have different perspectives
- Participate in a creative activity to engage the client

Materials
- Finger paint paper
- Paint – various colors; preferably in squirt/squeeze bottles

Description
The practitioner and client work together to make paint blots using paper and paint.

Allow the client to squirt paint of her/his color choice(s) onto the paper. Be careful not to put on too much paint or it may soak through the paper. The practitioner can make one at the same time or help the client as appropriate. Fold the paper in half allowing the paint to touch. Open the paper and see what the "paint spot" now looks like. Make three or four paint spots. In a group format, have each participant make one or two to allow for time to discuss all the pieces.

Discuss with the client what she/he thinks each paint spot looks like. This is not meant to be a projective test. The purpose is to have the client come up with different ideas about what the picture might look like. The practitioner can offer other suggestions as well. Suggestions for ways to look at the paint spots include:

- What do you see when you look at just one of the colors?
- What if you only look at a small part of the spot?
- What if you look at the spots on the paper that don't have paint?
- What does everyone else see? Do we see different things?

The goal is to convey that people see the same thing differently. Discuss how there were different things noticed even though it was the same paint spot. Relate this to social interactions. For example, "When you and your friends see something happen at school, you can see things differently even though it is the same situation." Or,

"When someone sees you do _____ and you mean one thing and they think it means something else, it could be like us looking at these paint spots." Continue the discussion with follow-up questions and topics that relate to the specific needs of the client.

Discussion

Many children and adolescents have difficulty recognizing how their peers and other adults see situations differently than they do themselves. This can result in confusion, misperception, and poor social interactions. These skills develop over time, but some individuals need more assistance in this area than others. Helping children and adolescents (and parents) recognize that people will sometimes see a situation, event, or a person's behavior in different ways can provide an opportunity to discuss misperceptions and ways of interpreting the behavior of others.

This activity can also be helpful for clients who are anxious and have difficulty seeing things in a different way in order to reduce anxiety. It can be used to reinforce the idea that things can be seen in various ways.

This activity is not designed as a projective test and the specific perceptions of the child and adolescent are not the focus of the activity. If there is concern with the perceptions provided by the client, the practitioner should consult with someone specialized in the use and interpretation of projective measures for further consideration.

About The Author

Kim D. O'Connor, M.Ed, is a Psychologist (Candidate Register) with a background in developmental and school psychology who maintains a private practice in Kentville, Nova Scotia. She offers counseling and assessment services to children, adolescents, and their parents to help them deal with various issues such as emotional and behavioral problems, learning disabilities, adjustment to life/family changes, parenting support, attention difficulties, social skills, and other related issues. Kim also acts as advocate for children in consultation with educators, parents, and interested individuals.

What's Under the Rock?
Source: Connie-Jean Latam

Theme: Social Skills
Recommended Age Range: Four to Nine
Treatment Modality: Individual, Group

Goals
- Increase socially appropriate behavior with peers
- Increase listening skills and respect for others' thoughts and feelings
- Participate in peer group activities in a cooperative manner
- Increase communication between client, peers, and therapist as trust is built

Materials
- One small box for each participant (Note: Consider adding several more boxes so the clients have a choice)
- Stickers
- A piece of blank paper
- Paper bag
- Rocks at least 3" in size
- Sand
- Leaves (dry or fresh), marbles, small toys, sea shells, stones, and other small interesting items
- Stickers, fruit, chips, candies

Advance Preparation
Use the stickers to number each of the boxes, numbering at least two more boxes than the number of participants in the group so they have a choice. Write numbers on a piece of paper; add one to two more than the number of participants in the group. (For example, if there are three participants, include numbers one to five.) Then cut the numbers into individual strips of paper and fold each in half. Place these folded pieces of paper in a paper bag.

Fill each box with sand, and bury in the sand at least one item, such as leaves (dry or fresh), marbles, small toys, sea shells, stones, or other small interesting items. Place a large rock on top of the item buried in the sand.

Place the numbered boxes (which are now filled with sand and with a rock on top) on a table in a way that makes them easy for participants to reach.

Description
The practitioner stars the game by asking each participant to pull a number from the paper bag that contains the numbered pieces of paper. Ask participants to

remember their numbers. Once all the participants have pulled out a number, ask them to put the numbers back into the paper bag. Each participant then goes to the box that matches the number she/he pulled. The participant looks in the box and under the rock. They are not to touch what is under the rock but only look at what they have found and decide what it is. The practitioner asks them to think about what it is: "Is what it is look obvious to you? What else does it look like?" Then tells them they will take a turn sharing with the others what they have found and describing what they think the object is or what it could be.

To begin the sharing, the practitioner pulls out a number from the paper bag and asks the participant with that number to go first. After the participant has spoken, the practitioner gives her/him a sticker or a piece of candy or fruit as a reward. Then that participant pulls a new number out of the paper bag and the participant with that number is the next one to speak. Continue this way until all participants have had a turn.

To use this exercise for an individual participant, place the numbered pieces of paper (from one to three) in the paper bag and have her/him pick a number. Then start the exercise. If it seems to help with communication, have the participant proceed with looking under the rock in the other boxes. Remember to be consistent with the rules and not to judge but only ask encouraging questions.

Discussion

This activity facilitates pro-social behavior and helps to build communication skills. A deeper level of awareness and communication can be encouraged by asking process questions such as, "What do you see under the rock?", "What made you think of this?", "Do you like what you see under the rock?" "Do you want to do something to the sand under the rock?", "Does this remind you of something?", etc.

The practitioner encourages each participant to talk about her/his findings, thoughts, and feelings. The practitioner does this by first asking the participant to tell his/her story while everyone is quiet and listens. If there seems to be a point of interest, the practitioner can encourage the participant to talk about it a bit more.

In a group environment, it is important to reinforce the following rules with the participants:

(1) Listen when someone else is talking.
(2) Patiently wait your turn.
(3) No teasing.
(4) No touching someone else's box.

The practitioner should also emphasize that the way a participant describes her/

121

his object is unique. There is no right or wrong in how one sees what is under the rock. Participants are not to judge whether they like or dislike the other participants' way of describing what they see under the rock. How each participant describes what she/he perceives to be under the rock is a personal expression, and this must be respected by everyone.

About the Author
Connie-Jean Latam, D.N.M., is a Doctor of Natural Medicine, accredited by the American Naturopathic Association, and a Certified Trauma and Loss Counsellor, Certified Addictions Counsellor, Certified Hypnotherapist, Certified Grief and Bereavement Counsellor, Certified Healing Touch, Therapeutic Touch Practitioner and Teacher, a Reiki Master, and a Theraplay® and Art Therapy practitioner. She is the author and illustrator of *Everything Is Food!* — a true story from the old soul of a three-year-old with a simple and profound message of "how to let go of life's challenges to find inner peace." Connie has been in private practice since 1990 serving adults, adolescents, and children. She owns the Art of Living Resource Centre Inc., located in Kingsville, Ontario.

So SORRY!
Source: Jodi Smith

Theme: Social Skills
Recommended Age Range: Eight to Thirteen
Treatment Modality: Individual, Group, Family

Goals
- Improve ability to accept responsibility for choices and actions
- Practice apologizing and repairing relationships following negative or inappropriate behaviors
- Explore and process feelings related to retaliation

Materials
- SORRY!™
- So SORRY! cards (included)
- Revenge! cards (included)
- Cardstock
- Scissors
- Stickers (optional)

Advance Preparation
Copy So SORRY! and Revenge! cards onto cardstock and cut.

Description
See instructions included with the SORRY!™ board game for general rules for game play. The only differences from the standard rules of play are as follow:

> Whenever a player BUMPS another player (by landing on her/his space or by drawing a So SORRY! card, that player also pulls a Revenge! card and responds to the question or statement on the card.

> Whenever a player SLIDES or enters a SAFETY ZONE, she/he selects a So SORRY! card and responds to the question or statement on the card.

The practitioner should decide ahead of time what the meaning of the wild card will be. The practitioner may wish to provide a treat or sticker for clients who choose this card or have the clients say something positive about themselves.

Discussion
Clients often have difficulty accepting responsibility for their actions and learning how to repair relationships following negative behaviors and interactions. Additionally, clients frequently present with behaviors related to "getting even,"

123

which may get them into trouble. The game SORRY!™ often elicits a playful "get even" response when a player bumps another player. The questions and scenarios in the game are hypothetical and non-threatening and enable clients to respond projectively.

The practitioner should use each of the provided cards as talking points and discussion prompts. The cards can be modified to meet the needs of the clients.

The Revenge! cards are meant to facilitate discussions about "getting even." They are not meant to condone, support, or encourage seeking revenge. They should provide the practitioner with opportunities to explore and redirect these feelings and behaviors.

About The Author

Jodi Smith, MSW, LCSW, RPT-S, is a Licensed Clinical Social Worker and Registered Play Therapist Supervisor specializing in using play therapy in clinical practice with children, adolescents and their families, as well as with adults. Jodi is currently the Director of Norton-Fisher Child & Family Programs for West End Family Counseling. Additionally, she maintains a private practice in Claremont, California, and is a part-time lecturer for the USC School of Social Work.

So SORRY! Cards

Take an extra turn!	Ask any player a question.
Joe and Carlos are playing handball. Joe accidentally hits Danny with the ball and laughs. Danny gets really upset and quits the game. What did Joe do wrong? What does he need to take responsibility for? How else could Carlos have handled this?	Jorge gets to school and realizes he has something in his pocket that he shouldn't have brought to school (for example, a lighter, pocket knife, toy gun). He had it in his pocket when he was at home and forgot about it. What should he do?
Robert is playing chase at recess when he accidentally runs into a classmate. He continues playing and forgets about what happened. The classmate becomes very upset and runs and tells a teacher. What is the problem? Who is to blame? How could the problem have been avoided?	Mark's little sister was bugging him all morning. She kept interrupting him while he was playing a computer game and made him lose! He was so frustrated, he hit her and she started crying. What did Mark do wrong? What does he need to take responsibility for? Who is to blame? What else could he have done?
WILD CARD	**WILD CARD**
Is it easy for you to say SORRY?	Practice saying SORRY and taking responsibility.

So SORRY! Cards

Who else do you know who has a hard time saying SORRY?	Talk about something you have done that you were really SORRY for? Did you get caught? Did you take responsibility?
Talk about a time you took responsibility for something you did wrong.	Talk about a time someone apologized to you. How did you feel afterwards? Did you forgive them?
Talk about a time you did something wrong and weren't SORRY.	How do you know if someone's apology is sincere?
How can you tell if someone is really SORRY for what they did?	Is there someone who you think owes you an apology? Why?
Is there something you do on a regular basis that you are SORRY for? (For example, talking back, not doing your chores, a bad habit?)	How do you accept someone's apology?

© Jodi Smith

So SORRY! Cards

Take an extra turn!	Ask any player a question.
How would someone know that you were really SORRY for something you did?	Have you ever taken responsibility for something you did not do? Why?
What stops you from taking responsibility and/or saying SORRY?	Is there anything you have done in the past that you have not apologized for, but would like to? Why haven't you?
WILD CARD	**WILD CARD**

Revenge! Cards

Talk about a time you got even with someone for something they did to you.	Do you know anyone who is always trying to "get even"?
How do YOU get even with someone?	Have you ever gotten even for something someone has done to you?
When someone makes you mad or hurts you, do you usually want to get back at them?	Say something about "getting even."
WILD CARD	**WILD CARD**
Does "getting even" make things better?	How can "getting even" create a problem?

Revenge! Cards

Do you worry about people wanting to get back at you?	Have you ever helped someone "get even"?
Is revenge a good thing? If so, under what circumstances?	Has anyone ever gotten back at you for something you have done to them?
Why do people always want to "get even"?	Have you ever had the opportunity to get back at someone and passed it up?
WILD CARD	**WILD CARD**

© Jodi Smith

How Would You Feel?
Source: Lynn R. Zakeri

Theme: Social Skills
Recommended Age Range: Eight to Eighteen
Treatment Modality: Individual

Goals
- Increase empathy
- Increase feeling vocabulary

Materials
- Paper
- Pencil or pen

Description
The practitioner introduces the activity by asking the client to identify she/he conflict she/he is having with someone or identify a strong negative feeling he/she has towards another person (feeling hurt, feeling left out, feeling jealous). The client is then asked, "How do you think ___ feels about this?" Or, "How do you think ___ would describe the situation?" (That is, the person she/he is having the conflict with). The practitioner then says to the client, "Write down what happened, but write as if you were the person you are having the conflict with."

When finished, the client is encouraged to read aloud what she/he has written. Further processing can take place, as well as an opportunity for further discussion of what was learned and experienced.

Discussion
The main aim of this activity is to strengthen the client's ability to empathize. This is an important life skill. Having the client put herself/himself into the other person's shoes helps the client to understand the other perspective and often results in the client rethinking her/his own actions. This activity also expands the client's feelings vocabulary and enables her/him to express various emotional states.

About The Author
Lynn R. Zakeri, LCSW, is a clinical social worker who has worked with children and adolescents for over ten years in private and educational settings. She has also published book reviews in professional journals.

Flip a Coin
Source: Liana Lowenstein

Theme: Social Skills
Recommended Age Range: Nine to Sixteen
Treatment Modality: Group

Goals
- Increase awareness of socially acceptable behavior
- Increase socially appropriate behavior with peers
- Provide opportunities for rehearsing social skills

Materials
- Coin
- Flip a Coin skits (included)

Advance Preparation
Photocopy the Flip a Coin skits onto colored card stock and cut out each skit. Write Heads on the back of each Heads skit card, and write Tails on the back of each Tails skit card.

Description
Divide the group into two teams. Have one team begin by flipping a coin. If that team flips a Head that team picks a skit from the Heads column on the skit sheet and acts it out. The other team then acts out the same skit, but follows the guidelines from the Tails column. Each skit must have a beginning, middle, and end. The activity continues in this manner until all five skits have been enacted. Team members can take turns being actors and directors. Afterwards, the leader facilitates a discussion by asking the following:

(1) What did you learn about inappropriate and appropriate behavior?
(2) How do others react when you behave in a way that is socially unacceptable?
(3) What did you learn today that you could try before the next session?

Discussion
This activity develops children's awareness of inappropriate and appropriate behaviors. It provides children with an opportunity to practice pro-social skills such as, being mature, assertive, and respectful. Psychodrama is used to engage children in the activity and to encourage creativity among the group members.

Reference
Lowenstein, L. (2002). *More creative interventions for children and youth.* Toronto, ON: Champion Press.

About The Author

Liana Lowenstein, MSW, RSW, CPT-S, is a social worker and Certified Play Therapy Supervisor in Toronto. She maintains a private practice, provides clinical supervision and consultation to mental health professionals, and lectures internationally on child and play therapy. She has authored numerous publications, including the books *Paper Dolls and Paper Airplanes: Therapeutic Exercises for Sexually Traumatized Children, Creative Interventions for Troubled Children and Youth, More Creative Interventions for Troubled Children and Youth, Creative Interventions for Bereaved Children, and Creative Interventions for Children of Divorce.*

Flip a Coin
Skits

HEADS	TAILS
Make up a skit about being at a birthday party and acting mature.	Make up a skit about being at a birthday party and acting silly.
Make up a skit about an argument with a friend in which you act assertive (you stand up for yourself in a non-violent way).	Make up a skit about an argument with a friend with whom you act aggressively.
Make up a skit in which you are playing a board game with a friend and you play by the rules.	Make up a skit in which you are playing a board game with a friend and you cheat in order to win the game.
Make up a skit about peer pressure in which you assert yourself (stand up for yourself in a respectful, non-violent way).	Make up a skit about peer pressure in which you give in to the pressure.
Make up a skit about treating other kids with respect.	Make up a skit about bullying other kids.

Hands Off! That's the Rule!

Source: Tammy Reis

Theme: Social Skills
Recommended Age Range: Four and Up
Treatment Modality: Individual, Group

Goals

- Decrease a child's use of physical aggression towards others
- Improve the child's understanding of personal space and boundaries

Materials

- Story: "Billy's Rule" (included)
- Box filled with various dinosaur figurines and other characters/toys that are relevant to the story
- Bag filled with small prizes (optional)

Advance Preparation

The practitioner should become familiar with the story and gather appropriate figurines that the child can use to enact the story as it is being read. Have a number of appropriate treats available that the child can choose from after reading the story and answering the questions.

Description

The practitioner introduces the story as follows:

"I am going to read you a story about a dinosaur named Billy. Sometimes Billy hurts other people when he is feeling frustrated, mad, or upset. He is learning a new rule to help him stop hurting other dinosaurs. While I read the story, you can use these figurines to act out the story. At the end of the story I have three questions to ask you about the story. If you are able to answer the questions, you can pick something from the prize bag."

After reading the story, the practitioner can ask the child the following questions, and award the child a prize for each correct response:

(1) What is the name of the T-rex in the story?
(2) What are some things that Billy likes to do?
(3) What is new rule that Billy learned?

It may be helpful to read this story over a number of sessions to help the child process and internalize the information.

Discussion

Bibliotherapy, or the purposeful use of books or stories in therapy, is an engaging and effective technique with children. The child will identify with Billy, the main character in this story, and the feelings he experiences.

The various scenarios in the story help the child to recognize situations in which aggressive behaviour occurs. The message, "Hands off! That's the rule!" is repeated throughout the story to reinforce for the child what is acceptable behaviour. Throughout the story, Billy is given the same message from his parents and teachers whenever he uses physical aggression with others. They tell him, "Hands off! That's the rule!" As the story progresses, Billy learns the rule and is able to integrate it into his thinking to avoid hurting others.

The characters in the story model appropriate behaviour for the child. In addition, the opportunity to act out the story with various figurines helps to reinforce the message in the story. Sharing this story with parents, foster parents, and teachers enables the caregivers to reiterate the messages outside of the therapy setting.

This story was written for a boy who loves dinosaurs. Characters and scenarios can and should be changed in the story to reflect the child's interests and circumstances.

About The Author

Tammy Reis, MSW, RSW, works for Child Abuse Treatment Services in the Yukon Territory as an outreach counsellor. She provides individual, group, and family counselling to children, youth and families in Northern communities. She is presently working towards her certification as a child and play therapist with the Canadian Association for Child and Play Therapy.

Story:
"Billy's Rule"

Once upon a time, there was a little dinosaur named Billy. Billy was a Tyrannosaurus Rex! He liked being a T-rex. Billy liked to laugh and make lots of noise. He liked running down hills as fast as he could. Billy liked chasing pterodactyls. He wished he could run and play all day!

Sometimes, like all dinosaurs, Billy would get angry. He would snort and stomp and roar and rave! This scared the other dinosaurs. Sometimes, Billy got so angry he would hit or bite or kick or slap! This hurt the other dinosaurs. This made Billy feel sad. He didn't like to hurt or scare other dinosaurs.

One day, Billy was playing in the sand at recess. Johnny was playing with Billy's favourite toy — a shiny shovel. Billy liked to dig and dig with that shovel. He made big piles in the sand!
    "Give me that shovel!" Billy yelled.
    "But I had it first," said Johnny.
    Billy pushed Johnny. He took the shovel and ran away. Johnny cried and cried. Billy's teacher saw Billy push Johnny.
    "Billy! Hands off! That's the rule!" said the teacher. Billy gave the shovel back to Johnny. He had to stand with his teacher for the rest of recess.

One night, Billy was chasing pterodactyls. He was having fun! Running and jumping and laughing with the giant birds. Sam, Billy's pet, was playing too!
    "Billy, its time to get ready for bed!" his mother called.
    "NO!!!!" Billy roared. He wanted to play! He was angry! Billy pulled Sam's tail very hard.
    "Billy. Hands off! That's the rule!" said his mother. Billy went to bed without a snack. He was hungry from all that running.

One time at school, Billy was playing dodge ball in the gym. He was running and throwing the ball with his friends. Billy was excited! When Billy ran by his teacher, he slapped the teacher's bum. That's a private part.
    "Billy. Hands off! That's the rule!" the gym teacher said.
Billy had to sit out for the rest of the game. It's not okay to touch people's privates.

The other day, the teacher was teaching the ABCs. But Billy wanted to play.
    "Come sit with the other children, Billy," the teacher asked.

"No!!!!" Billy roared. Billy was angry. He wanted to play. Billy raised his hand to hit his teacher.

"Billy. Hands off! That's the rule!" his teacher said.

Billy stopped.

"Hands off! That's the rule!" he reminded himself. Billy didn't hit his teacher.

"That's right. You know the rule." She smiled at Billy. Billy sat down with his friends. He learned the letter "H". Billy liked to learn new things. Hand starts with "H." Hands off! That's the rule!

Later that day, Billy was playing with his friends. He wanted to play tag. Nelly and Johnny didn't. They wanted to play hide and seek. Billy was angry! He wanted to play tag. Billy wanted to hit Johnny! But then he remembered…

"Hands off! That's the rule!" Billy said to himself. Instead of hitting Johnny, Billy smiled.

"Can we play tag after?" Billy asked.

"Sure!" said Nelly and Johnny.

Billy, Nelly, and Johnny ran and played all afternoon. They had fun. Billy was very proud of himself. He didn't hit anyone. Hands off! That's the rule! Billy liked that rule!

© Tammy Reis

137

Friendship Fruit Salad
Source: Sarah Wells

Theme: Social Skills
Recommended Age Range: Four to Six
Treatment Modality: Group

Goals
* Increase vocabulary around friendship
* Learn and practice pro-social behavior with peers
* Increase group cohesion through fun and cooperation

Material
* Assorted fruit (grapes, bananas, pears, apple, kiwi)
* Cutting board
* Knife
* Mixing bowl
* Serving bowls
* Spoons

Advance preparation
Purchase a selection of fruit and collect materials for preparing and serving the fruit salad.

Description
A large bowl of assorted fruits is placed in front of the group. The activity is introduced by saying that the group is going to make a special fruit salad. The group leader then begins reading the following story:

The Special Fruit Salad

There once were all these different fruits that were being made into the special food for an upcoming party. Each of the fruits thought that they were the most special ingredients to the salad. What they did not know is that the cook was cutting and mixing all the fruits together in something called fruit salad. This caused a lot of arguing among the fruits since they did not think the other fruits were as special as they were. They thought that the grapes would not taste very good because they were too small, and the pears were a funny color — who would want to eat them? And the kiwi was just a weird looking fruit all together.

As the story is being told, the group leader takes each fruit one by one and cuts it into pieces, adding each one to the large serving bowl. The group leader can make up descriptions about the other fruit being added, depending on what fruit is chosen for the activity, to fit the theme that friends come in different shapes and sizes.

The group shares the fruit salad, and the group leader makes a statement about sharing, such as, "We are sharing this delicious fruit salad—everyone gets some, because it is nice to share." As group members are given a share of fruit salad, each one must say "Thank you."

Then the rest of the story is read aloud:

Well, the guests loved the special fruit salad. It was the best thing that they had ever tasted. They loved the taste of the kiwi and shape of the grapes and the color of the pears. They thought that all the fruits tasted so good together and that they were even more special then when they were by themselves. The guests decided to call this special fruit salad, friendship fruit salad.

When the story is finished, the leader asks the group, "What did the people think of the fruit salad?" The following process questions can be asked to facilitate discussion:

(1) How is this story like the friendships we have?
(2) What makes a good friend?
(3) When you meet someone new, how can you become friends with that person?
(4) What is special about each person in this group?
(5) What did we learn today about sharing?
(6) What did we learn today about good manners?

Discussion

The storytelling part to this activity provides a symbolic distance to the topic of making friends. If friendship is an area that children are struggling with, this distance may make the discussion less difficult. This activity leads the children into discussions about what a friend is and what characteristics they hope to find in a friend. There is always a piece of fruit that the children have never tried before and this leads to discussion about the friends we have not met yet and how we can meet new friends. The leader can highlight that other children may look or act mean and unfriendly, but when you get to know them they are nice and you have a lot in common with them. Children's feelings and abilities in the area of making friends and keeping friends can be assessed and monitored through the group discussion.

About The Author

Sarah Wells, BA, works as an adult and child group facilitator at Merrymount Children's Centre in London, Ontario. Sarah specializes in working with high-risk families. She has completed both the Canadian Association for Child and Play Therapy (CACPT) certificate program and Trauma and Loss Specialist certificate.

© Sarah Wells

141

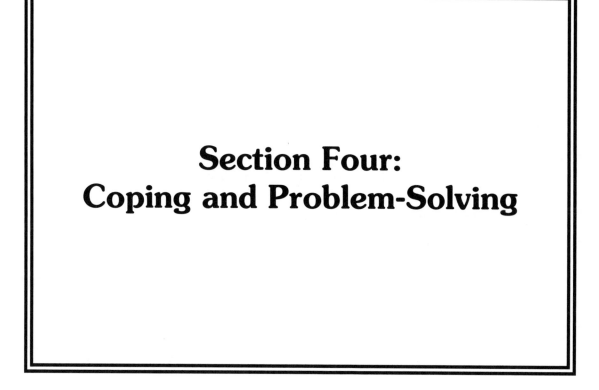

Section Four:
Coping and Problem-Solving

Sweet Dream Box
Source: Chrissy Snead

Theme: Coping and Problem-Solving
Recommended Age Range: Three to Ten
Treatment Modality: Individual, Family

Goals
- Allow for expression of feelings related to fears and worries
- Reduce/eliminate nightmares

Materials
- Paper
- Crayons or markers
- Scissors
- Shoebox or Ziploc® bag

Description
Begin by asking the child to talk about the nightmares or fears she/he experiences at night. The practitioner then has the parent and child work together to create a sweet dream box. The parent and child come up with a list of sweet dreams for the child to have. These can be special family memories, fun things that the child likes to do, or favorite characters the child would like to meet. Have them write out the dreams on a piece of paper and cut them out. Then they can decorate a shoebox (cutting a hole in the top) to put the dreams in, or they can put the dreams into a zip-lock bag. Each night before the child goes to bed, the parent and child will pull out a sweet dream from the box or bag and that will create a sense of safety and calm.

If the child wakes up during the night from a bad dream, she/he can be encouraged to think about the sweet dream.

Discussion
Many children have nightmares or fears related to nighttime. They have difficulty coping with these worries and often experience unrealistic fears. This activity uses cognitive behavioral therapy to help alleviate these fears, and as well develops the parent-child relationship. Children and parents will enjoy thinking of fun things they have done together. Children will be excited to talk about the good dreams they are having.

About The Author
Chrissy Snead, M.Ed., LPC, is a licensed professional counselor in Birmingham, Alabama. She works with children and adolescents and has over seven years of

clinical experience. She utilizes a variety of play therapy techniques when working with her clients. She also enjoys attending seminars related to play therapy. In November 2007, Chrissy gave a presentation to her fellow colleagues on using play therapy with patients who have obsessive-compulsive disorder.

© Chrissy Snead

Bedtime Beads
Source: Natalie Caufield

Theme: Coping and Problem-Solving
Recommended Age Range: Three to Sixteen
Treatment Modality: Individual, Family

Goals
- Teach and implement relaxation skills
- Increase positive thoughts about self
- Increase communication between caregiver and child

Materials
- Large and small (preferably darker color) wooden beads
- Paints, permanent markers, or small stickers
- String

Description
The client is asked to choose several large and small wooden beads. The practitioner explains that the large beads represent those things that give the child or youth positive feelings. The client may think of images of people, places, objects, or animals, or use inspirational words like love, gratitude, hope, and dreams. The client writes a word or draws a symbol onto the large beads using the paints, permanent markers, or small stickers. Younger children will need assistance. After working with each large bead, the client discusses the positive emotion that is linked to the symbol or the word she/he has made.

The process continues until the client has a number of decorated beads. The smaller, darker beads are the "breath beads." The "breath beads" follow the large beads and encourage the client to pause and take several deep breaths as a way to allow the word, symbol or emotion from the large bead to resonate with her/him. The beads are strung in a pattern that alternating between the large (emotion) and small (breath) beads. The ends of the string are then tied together.

The client may use the beads independently at bedtime or during stressful times. The client may choose to place the beads on the night table or under the pillow so they remain close to her/him. The bedtime beads can also become a nighttime ritual with a caregiver. The caregiver listens to the child describe the meaning of the beads or may create additional words or symbols that represent her/his positive feelings for the child.

Discussion
Bedtime can be difficult for children and youth who struggle with problems, who are

worried or who experience intrusive thoughts from past trauma. During the day we busy our bodies and minds but, at night, without the distractions of daytime activities, issues are more likely to surface. This activity emphasizes the mind-body connection by helping the client to experience pleasant thoughts and feelings and to integrate those feelings into the body through breath work. This will help to minimize the intrusive thoughts and negative feelings.

About The Author

Natalie Caufield, MSW, RSW, is a social worker in Sudbury, Ontario. She maintains a private practice and works for the Domestic Violence/Sexual Assault Treatment Program at the Sudbury Regional Hospital. Natalie is a play therapy intern with the Canadian Association of Child and Play Therapy.

My Favorite Things
Source: Cyndi Starzyk-Frey

Theme: Coping and Problem-Solving
Recommended Age Range: Six to Sixteen
Treatment Modality: Individual, Group

Goals
- Teach the concept of positive self-care
- Implement healthy coping strategies

Materials
- Lyrics for "My Favorite Things"© by Rodgers and Hammerstein
- Colored paper
- Magazines
- Glue stick
- Craft supplies
- Crayons (or pencil crayons, felts, etc.)

Advance Preparation
Make individual paper visuals of each of the "favorite things" in the lyrics by using the craft supplies, magazines, and colored paper. For example, "girls in white dresses with blue satin sashes" would have a page with a magazine picture or drawing of girls in white dresses.

Description
Begin by reading the lyrics or listening to the song "My Favorite Things." As each line is sung or read, the accompanying picture is held up.

Next, discuss the importance of having favorite things that help us feel better. This discussion leads to the clients talking about their favorite things. They then make their own pages using magazines, crayons, and craft supplies to depict their favorite things. Discuss each favorite thing and explore ways to incorporate these things into the clients' lives.

Discussion
This activity provides a creative way for clients to engage in self-care. For clients who enjoy using the computer, pictures of favorite things can be searched for on the Internet. Clients can use these images to create their own PowerPoint

presentations. This activity is engaging and taps into the clients' imaginations.

Follow-up sessions should explore ways in which the clients have used their "favorite things" to help themselves feel better in times of need.

About The Author
Cyndi Starzyk-Frey, M.Ed., RSW, is a social worker in Lethbridge, Alberta. She maintains a private practice, provides clinical supervision, and teaches at Lethbridge College. She gives workshops and presentations on child therapy, particularly in the area of trauma and self-care. In her leisure time she acts, directs and writes plays, and incorporates expressive arts into her therapy practice.

© Cyndi Starzyk-Frey

Hug
Source: Ceilidh Eaton Russell

Theme: Coping and Problem Solving
Recommended Age Range: Three to Adult
Treatment Modality: Individual, Family

Goals
- Increase open communication about feelings
- Increase comfort among family members
- Assess and increase family members skills in supporting one another

Materials
- Fabric (approximately 8 to 12 inches wide, 3 to 5 feet long)
- Markers
- Fabric paints
- Scissors
- Needle and thread
- Beads, sequins, ribbons, or other decorative materials

Description
Lay a piece of fabric out on a flat surface. Although any soft fabric will work, using a sheet used by or an article of clothing belonging to a special person can add an extra meaningful and personal touch to this activity.

Ask the child to reach her/his arms out to the sides on top of the fabric and use a marker to trace her/his arms and hands onto the fabric. After both arms have been traced, the child can connect the lines so that it resembles a scarf with hands on each end. With help from adults as appropriate, the child can cut out her/his "hug" along the traced outline or not, based on preference.

To "infuse" the hug with meaning, the child can draw, paint, glue, or sew images, words, or decorations onto the hug. Favorite memories, wishes, feelings, sayings, symbols, or other meaningful images or words may be included so that the child's messages and feelings can be with her/his loved one all the time.

Discussion
Both the final product and the process of making a "hug" have therapeutic value for children, teenagers, and adults in a broad range of situations. Children can benefit from having a special hug as a familiar, comforting item while they are struggling with separation anxiety, hospitalization or medical procedures, parents who are separated or divorced, a family member or loved one who is travelling or moving away, or if they are moving to a new place or even into foster care. When

a caregiver or other significant person in a child's life is hospitalized or dying, children or teenagers can make hugs for that person, or the adult may create one to give to the child or teen. Some families have put their hugs in the casket of a loved one after she/he has died.

Children often feel more comfortable expressing themselves while focusing on a creative activity. While creating a hug, there is a great opportunity for meaningful discussion about memories; recognizing special connections among loved ones; exploring how those connections exist even when people are not physically together; and helping children see that sharing emotional support is a wonderful way of helping and caring for others.

Reference
Eaton Russell, C. (2007). *Living dying: A guide for adults supporting grieving children and teenagers*. Toronto, ON: Max and Beatrice Wolfe Centre for Children's Grief and Palliative Care.

About The Author
Ceilidh Eaton Russell, BA, CLSt. Dip., is a Certified Child Life Specialist and Grief Counselor in Toronto, Ontario. Ceilidh provides clinical support to children and families living with the dying and death of a loved one at the Max and Beatrice Wolfe Centre for Children's Grief and Palliative Care at Mount Sinai Hospital. She teaches for the Child Life Studies Program at McMaster University in Hamilton, and conducts research through the Hospital for Sick Children in Toronto, exploring family communication when a child is dying. Ceilidh is the author of *Living Dying: A Guide for Adults Supporting Grieving Children and Teenagers*.

Care Tags
Source: Jodi Smith

Theme: Coping and Problem-Solving
Recommended Age Range: Thirteen and Up
Treatment Modality: Individual, Group, Family

Goals
- Increase self-awareness
- Improve positive and clear communication
- Increase ability to appropriately express needs

Materials
- Construction paper cut into the shape of a tag (see template)

Description
Begin with a discussion of how everyone expresses her/his feelings differently (give examples: "Some people cry when they are sad, some shut down, others look/act angry"). Additionally, different people want/need different things when they feel different emotions (give examples: "Some people want to be left alone when they are sad, others want a hug or to talk"). Begin to process how everyone is different, and that we cannot assume that everyone knows what we are feeling or knows what we need from her/him. Explain that people are not like clothes or other things that come with care tags or instruction manuals.

Explain the activity as follows:

"Wouldn't it be nice if everyone came with a care tag that told others exactly how to take care of them (give examples of clothing care tags such as 'Delicate,' 'Dry clean only,' and 'Handle with care')? In order to do that, we first need to understand the link between our own behaviors, feelings, and needs. We are going to create several care tags that will help you better understand your feelings, communicate to others what you are feeling, and identify what you need from them (or yourself) when you are feeling that way. On the back of each care tag, you can draw a picture that either represents that feeling or something that makes you feel that way."

Each care tag will say: "When I _____ (behavior, action, or situation), I am feeling _____ (emotion), and I need _____."

Discussion
For many clients this can be a very difficult activity. Have the client begin with a feeling with which she/he is comfortable before moving on to more intense or

sensitive emotions. This activity also works well if the client has entered the session expressing a problem that easily fits this format (i.e., "I had a really bad day at school yesterday and I just needed a little time alone, but my mom wanted me to go with her to the store"). The practitioner can then work with the client to break this down on the care tag ("How would your mom know you were mad?"). It is generally easier for the client to start with the feeling, then move to how others will know when they are feeling that emotion, and end with what she/he needs. When completed, discuss the possibility of sharing these care tags with her/his parents. If possible, and if the client is in agreement, arrange for the parents to join the session and support the client in sharing the care tags.

This activity easily adapts to family sessions, with each family member creating their own "tags" and then sharing them with the family.

About The Author

Jodi Smith, MSW, LCSW, RPT-S, is a Licensed Clinical Social Worker and Registered Play Therapist Supervisor specializing in using play therapy in clinical practice with children, adolescents and their families, as well as with adults. Jodi is currently the Director of Norton-Fisher Child & Family Programs for West End Family Counseling. Additionally, she maintains a private practice in Claremont, California, and is a part-time lecturer for the USC School of Social Work.

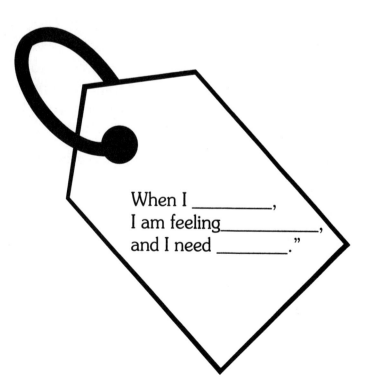

When I _____,
I am feeling_____,
and I need _____."

Dump It on the Queen/King
Source: Leahanne Prolas

Theme: Coping and Problem-Solving
Recommended Age Range: Eight and Up
Treatment Modality: Group

Goals
- To work together as a team to solve problems
- Increase communication within the group

Materials
- Decorative box
- Crown

Description
The group leader shows the group members an attractively decorated small box and a crown. The leader explains to the group members that throughout the group sessions, if they have any problems that they would like help in solving, they can write it out on a piece of paper (without signing their names) and put it in the box. The group leader describes the expression "Dump it on the Queen/King" as meaning that any problems the kingdom is having can be brought forth to the Queen/King and ask her/him to solve them.

The group members take turns being the Queen or King. They sit on the throne and wear the crown. A problem is taken from the box and read aloud to the group. The Queen/King explains to the group what she/he would do to solve the problem and then asks the group (their Royal Subjects) for their recommendations. When the problem has been sufficiently resolved, a new Queen/King is chosen and a new problem is discussed.

Discussion
Group members enjoy sitting on the throne and wearing the crown. It enables group members who are shy to bring forth problems that they are facing without the fear of being singled out or without feeling embarrassed.

This activity can cover a wide variety of issues while addressing a number of goals. The group members are working as a team, communicating, and problem- solving. Risk-taking is often involved for some group members. The group members are given a chance to share their thoughts and feelings in a non-threatening way.

It is recommended that this activity be done in later sessions when the group members have acquired skills through previous sessions that will help them with problem-solving.

<u>About The Author</u>

Leahanne Prolas, M.Ed., is a children's group facilitator and counselor in Ottawa, Ontario. She received her B.Ed. and M.Ed. at McGill University in Montreal, Quebec and has spent many years teaching children with special needs in the classroom.

Even Superheroes Have Problems
Source: Lawrence C. Rubin

Theme: Coping and Problem-Solving
Recommended Age Range: Five to Eighteen
Treatment Modality: Individual, Group

Goals
- Use fantasy to develop solutions to daily life problems (young children)
- Encourage positive reframing of problems as surmountable obstacles (older children and teens)

Materials
- For younger children: arts and crafts supplies, including crayons and paper, clay, and papier-mâché materials
- For older children and teens: drawing materials, Internet access to song lyrics, and free downloadable programs such as Second Life® or Hero Machine in which avatars can be created

Description
The goal for both age groups is similar: to pose a question or series of questions to encourage clients to imagine themselves as a superhero with powers to solve a problem they are experiencing. Younger children are asked to consider which of the powers they would like to have if they were a superhero, and then to draw (or use clay to represent) themselves as the superhero. Older children and teens may also use these materials, but can also select lyrics from favorite songs or create avatars of themselves in either Second Life® (www.secondlife.com) or Hero Machine (www.ugo.com/channels/comics/heroMachine/classic.asp).

The questions are as follows:

- What would you do if you could fly?
- What would you do if you could move at super speed?
- What would you do if you could travel through time?
- What would you do if you could change shape?
- What would you do if you could run super fast?
- What would you do if you could have super strength?
- What would you do if you could be invisible?
- What would you do if you could commit crimes without detection?
- What would you do if you could read someone else's mind?
- What would you do if you could save someone in trouble?

As the clients make their superhero (regardless of the chosen medium), the practitioner encourages them to discuss the power and how it could be used to solve a particular problem in their lives. Younger clients may remain in the metaphor by talking about the problem as if it were occurring in the life of the superhero, while older children and teens are encouraged to somehow transform the supersolution into one that would work in their own lives.

For example, a teen who wants to work up the courage to ask someone out on a date could create an avatar in Hero Machine that changes shape, and then rehearse with the practitioner how to change the way she/he can present herself/himself to that person. The teen may also use lyrics to an existing song or compose her/his own "superhero song of encouragement and self-confidence." A younger client, who is afraid of sleeping in her/his own room, can imagine being invisible, so that if a monster comes into the room while she/he is asleep, the monster won't see her/him.

Discussion

Children, both young and old, get stuck trying to solve problems. Collaborative fantasy and imaginary exercises, using word, song lyrics or manipulative images can provide a "zone of proximal development" in which solutions can be created and practiced. The metaphor of superpowers can function as a launching platform for these solutions, which can then be practiced in the clients' "real" lives.

References

Rubin, L. (2006). *Using superheroes in counseling and play therapy.* New York: Springer.

Vygotsky, L.S. (1978). *Mind in society.* Cambridge, MA: Harvard University Press.

About The Author

Lawrence C. Rubin, Ph.D., LMHC, RPT-S, is a licensed Psychologist, Mental Health Counselor, and Registered Play Therapist (Supervisor) in private practice, as well as Professor of Counselor Education at St. Thomas University in Miami, Florida. Current president of the Florida Association for Play Therapy, Dr. Rubin has co-authored several articles on play therapy, and has edited several books in the area of popular culture and counseling, the most recent of which are *Using Superheroes in Counseling and Play Therapy* and *Popular Culture in Counseling: Psychotherapy and Play-based Interventions.*

Safe Place Sand Tray

Source: Barbara Jones Warrick

Theme: Coping and Problem-Solving
Recommended Age Range: Seven and Up
Treatment Modality: Individual

Goals
- Identify a safe place and the associated thoughts and feelings
- Implement healthy coping strategies

Materials
- Sand tray
- Sand tray objects (representing various categories: people, animals, plants, buildings, vehicles, etc.)
- Camera
- Writing materials

Description
Advise the client that as you begin to work through her/his trauma and fear that you will start by helping them to feel safer. To get started, ask the client to build a safe place in the sand tray. It may be real or imaginary.

When the client is finished, ask her/him to tell you about her/his safe place. As the client speaks, write down "the story" of the safe place by using her/his words as much as possible. You may ask questions to gather more information about the experience of safety. It is important to start and finish the story as follows:

Title: _____'s safe place (use the client's name).
First line: This is _____'s safe place.
Final line: This is a safe place. This is _____'s safe place.

Read the story back to the client, making any additions or changes she/he noted. Then tell the client you are going to help them her/him move the safe place into her/his body. Teach the client how to do a self-hug by stating, "Cross your arms over your heart so that your hands rest on the opposite shoulders, then hug yourself.

Ask the client to look at the safe place. Have the client continue the self-hug while you read the story. This may be repeated two to three times. Take two photographs of the sand tray and make a copy of the story. Give one photo and the story to the client. Advise her/him to practice looking at the safe place picture while doing the self-hug even when she/he does not feel stressed or afraid until it becomes automatic.

At the end of the session invite the client's caregiver into the room to share the new skill. Engage the caregiver as a story reader/coach.

Keep the other photo and copy of the story for future sessions. Use this resource when the client engages in work that is stressful or fear-inducing.

Discussion

By building a safe place in the sand, the client immediately has a nurturing experience. The building of the safe place and telling of the story provides the client with opportunities to identify feelings; particularly those related to fear and safety. It also allows the practitioner to assess the client's strengths and needs in this area. The telling and retelling of the story, practicing the self-hug and the ability to take the story with them strengthens the client's emotional resources and overall sense of safety. By keeping a copy of the photo and story for later use, the practitioner can continue supporting the client through difficult work.

<u>About The Author</u>

Barbara Jones Warrick, M.Ed., CPT-S, is a graduate of the M.Ed. Counseling program at the University of Western Ontario. She is a child and family therapist working in private practice and agency settings, and she is a Certified Child and Play Therapist Supervisor with the Canadian Association for Child and Play Therapy and the International Board of Examiners of Certified Play Therapists. She has completed the training with Gisela Schubach De Domenico in Sand Tray World Play and has also completed training in the Erica Method with Mararetta Sjolund. She teaches sand tray therapy and uses sand tray extensively in her work with children, families, groups, and individuals.

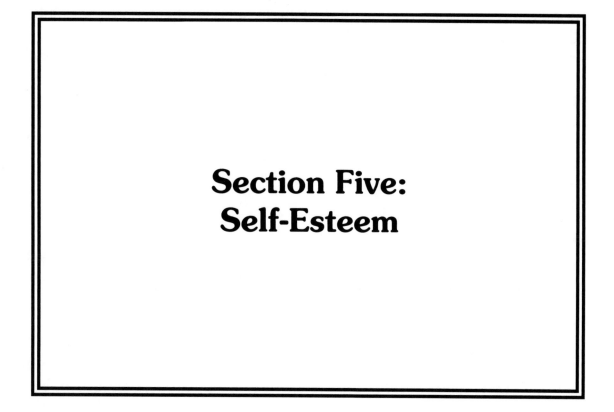

Section Five:
Self-Esteem

Self-Esteem Booster
Source: Amy Brace

Theme: Self-Esteem
Recommended Age Range: Four and Up
Treatment Modality: Individual, Family, Group

Goals
- Increase self-esteem (based on client self-reporting and/or observable affect)
- Demonstrate positive communication skills (by effectively teaching a skill to another)
- Practice interpersonal attunement (via assessing/sharing necessary feedback)

Materials
- Accessories identified by the client, for example, a football, foosball, art supplies, musical instrument (if specialized items are not available in your office, the client can bring the item to the session)
- Poster board or construction paper (optional)
- Camera (optional)

Advance Preparation
If a prop is needed, make a plan to obtain the item either by the practitioner having the item(s) in the office or asking the client to bring it to the session.

Description
The practitioner shares a strong interest, intense curiosity, and enthusiastic desire to learn a skill that the client possesses. The practitioner says that she/he would like the client to teach him/her the client's skill or area of expertise. The practitioner may already be aware through working with the client what his/her interests/hobbies/skills are; but, if not, the practitioner can ask the client for a specific description. This intervention can be structured and planned for a specific session or can occur spontaneously given sufficient time and available props. For example, if the client begins talking about a skill or hobby, the practitioner can then ask for step-by-step instructions on how to perform the skill or the practitioner can plan to address this later in a specific session.

The practitioner introduces the activity by speaking with the client about one of her/his skills. The practitioner remains very curious and inquisitive about every little detail of the skill regardless of their current knowledge of the skill. For instance, a client may enjoy football and thus the practitioner may ask to be taught how to throw a football or how to play the game. The practitioner should be as specific as possible about what he/she would like to learn. For example, if the intention is to have the client teach the practitioner how to throw the football, the client can demonstrate how to hold the football, where to place one's fingers on the football, the angle at which to throw, the body motion to use when throwing, and so on. Once the client teaches one aspect of the skill, the practitioner can ask a question leading to another level of specificity.

The teaching occurs on a verbal level but also on a sensory level as the client will ultimately physically demonstrate the skill. The practitioner will ask for demonstrations of the skill in an attempt to learn as much as possible and comment on many details. The practitioner will use the observation time to learn the skill and attempt to mimic the skill, asking for feedback on her/his progress. This will lead to more teaching followed possibly by further demonstration by the client and then further inquiries and practice by the practitioner.

The client can also teach the skill to parent(s) who would need to be prepped on following the child's lead in teaching. The parent would also need to be encouraged to hold as much curiosity with as many specific questions as possible about the skill and how to learn it. The same would be true for use in a group setting, as group members would have to show respect for one other.

Once the skill is adequately taught and learned to the client's satisfaction, then it may be incorporated into a joint play activity either during a session or at home with the client's parents. A picture can also be taken in the session of the client performing his/her skill and put on a poster board or construction paper for the client to take home.

Discussion

Many children in therapy have low self-esteem. They have difficulty feeling competent and knowledgeable given their personal/familial struggles. This activity gives them an opportunity to experience being an expert. The activity allows the client to practice her/his communication skills, social skills, and relationship building. The teaching experience requires both the "teacher" and the "student" to be attuned to each other in order to perform the activity. Clients enjoy this activity and leave the session feeling empowered.

About The Author

Amy Brace, LMSW, ACSW, is a clinical social worker in Grand Rapids, Michigan. She is employed as an outpatient therapist where she specializes in play therapy and the treatment of traumatized children and their families. She also works at a psychiatric hospital as a group leader for teenagers and adults. She assisted with the development and implementation of a treatment program entitled "ADOPTS: Experiential Model: Trauma Informed Therapy for Pre- and Post-Adoptive Children" that is used on a national level by Bethany Christian Services, an international adoption/social service agency.

The Colors of Me
Source: Katherine Arkell

Theme: Self-Esteem
Recommended Age Range: Six and Up
Treatment Modality: Individual

Goals
- Gather information about client's strengths and feelings about self
- Increase positive feelings about self

Materials
- Assorted colors of sand (6-10 different colors suggested)
- Small, clear plastic bottle (approx. 4-5 inches in height) with lid (usually found in same aisle as sand in craft store)
- Small funnel
- Colored index card

Advance Preparation
Write "Good Things About Me" at the top of the index card.

Description
Provide the child with a bottle and an index card. Explain the activity as follows:

"We are going to talk about good things about you today. I would like you to tell me something positive about yourself or something you are good at with each color of sand you pour into your bottle. I will write each one on the index card so when you are done you will have a record of what each color represents."

As transcriber, the practitioner writes down the name of each color (in the order it is poured into the bottle) followed by a description in the child's own words. For example, "Blue – I'm good at math."

Once the child has filled the bottle with sand and identified positive traits about self, the practitioner processes the activity by asking the following questions: (1) Where might you put this in your house/room? (2) Who might you share it with? (3) What other strengths could you include if the bottle had more room? (Stress this point to the child: "This is by no means a complete list, only a reminder of some of the great things about you!")

At the end of the activity, the child takes home the filled bottle with the completed card.

Discussion

Some children struggle with identifying personal strengths. They will often ask, "What do you think I should say?" What do you think I am good at?" etc. The practitioner should avoid giving direct responses, but instead offer "hints" by asking the child, "I wonder what your teacher would say you are good at?" or "I wonder what kind of friend your friends think you are?" and so on.

Some children keep their sand intact for a layered look. Others like to slightly swish the colors together, and still others like to shake it up so all the colors are combined.

This activity can be adapted for grief/anger/anxiety issues. For example, the child identifies special memories about the person who died with each color of sand poured into the bottle, or identifies healthy ways to deal with anger or anxiety.

About The Author

Katherine Arkell, MSW, LCSW, works as an outpatient therapist at Vista Health in Bentonville, Arkansas, serving children ages 6–18 and their families. She is currently working towards completing her Registered Play Therapist Supervisor credentials. Her practice areas of interest include anxiety, depression, grief and blended families.

Positive Postings
Source: Jacqueline Melissa Swank

Theme: Self-Esteem
Recommended Age Range: Six and Up
Treatment Modality: Individual, Family, or Group

Goals
- Improve self-esteem by identifying and expressing positive qualities about oneself through writing/drawing and verbalization
- Promote positive interactions with others through a discussion about one's positive qualities with the practitioner or other group members, family members, etc.
- Promote positive self-talk through verbalization of positive self-qualities

Materials
- Construction paper
- Crayons/markers, colored pencils
- Post-it® Notes/sticky notes, or different shapes of paper and tape

Description
The practitioner may choose to begin the activity by reading a book about self-esteem. Then the practitioner asks the client to draw an outline of her/his body (or a pre-drawn outline can be available for the client). When providing a pre-drawn outline, the client can still personalize the outline by drawing onto it her/his face or other personal features. Then the practitioner asks the client to think about positive qualities about herself/himself and write each one on a Post-it® Note. When the client is finished, the practitioner has the client read them aloud and then stick them to her/his outline. The practitioner may also give "positive notes" to the client or have family members, teachers, etc. involved in this process give her/him positive notes.

When the activity is completed, the practitioner processes the experience with the client. The practitioner may say, "You really worked hard on this activity. I wonder how you feel about making positive postings. Think about a time when you thought negative things about yourself or felt angry, frustrated, or disappointed with yourself. How could your 'positive postings' help you?"

Variation
This activity can be modified for a group or family session. Members can give compliments on sticky notes to each other.

Discussion
This activity provides clients with the opportunity to focus on their strengths,

instead of focusing on the problem areas. This is especially useful with families or groups that constantly focus on each others' negative qualities. Young clients enjoy using the "sticky" notes and the practitioner can help them write or draw on the notes if needed. Clients can place the positive notes in a special place to look at when they are having a difficult time thinking about positive qualities about themselves.

Some clients may have difficulty identifying positive qualities about themselves. The practitioner may need to provide some examples to help these clients get started with the activity. Additionally, the practitioner can use this hesitation to facilitate a discussion about how the clients view themselves. Furthermore, the practitioner may want to begin with a small body outline and switch to a larger outline if several qualities are identified by the clients.

About The Author

Jacqueline M. Swank is a Licensed Clinical Social Worker and a Registered Play Therapist. Currently, she is a doctoral student in Counselor Education at the University of Central Florida in Orlando and works part-time at a psychiatric hospital for children and adolescents in Daytona Beach, Florida. She has worked in a variety of therapeutic settings with children and adolescents and their families, including residential, inpatient, partial hospitalization, and outpatient settings. She has written about innovative techniques and presented nationally and internationally at conferences.

Two Faces

Source: Kimberly Blackmore

Theme: Self-Esteem
Recommended Age Range: Ten and Up
Treatment Modality: Individual

Goals
- Increase positive verbalizations about self
- Increase awareness of one's own personal interests, dreams, or talents
- Identify the connection between having a sense of belonging to a group while still remaining an individual

Materials
- Two Styrofoam heads (Styrofoam heads can be purchased at Value Village)
- Magazine pictures
- Glue stick
- Scissors

Advance Preparation
Cut the two Styrofoam heads in half and glue back together so that the head now has two faces.

Description
The practitioner begins by discussing with the child how we tend to see ourselves much differently than how others see us. The child is encouraged to use the head to depict on one side a face that represents what she/he allows the world to see and, on the other side, a face she/he keeps hidden from others. The practitioner and child then compare the two perceptions.

The child decorates the two faces by cutting out various pictures or words from magazines to form a collage. The child chooses pictures or words that represent what the outside world sees and glues those to one of the faces of the Styrofoam head. On the opposite face, the child chooses pictures or words that represent who he/she is on the inside.

This concept will allow the child to better understand what identity she/he attempts to show to the world as compared with what her/his true personality may be. A discussion around peer pressure, self-esteem, and a sense of belonging may be processed further.

Discussion
The purpose of this activity is to help the child identify and understand her/his

self-concept, how past experiences and other individuals can have an impact on her/his self-esteem, and what the child chooses to reveal with regards to her/his true personality, strengths, interests, talents, dreams, or wishes. Often if a child experiences little encouragement or is labeled negatively by others, this will affect the child's self-esteem, the persona she/he decides to show others, and who/where the child will go to find acceptance.

About The Author
Kimberly Blackmore, M.C., is a Play Therapy Intern with Branching Out Therapeutic Services in Brampton, Ontario. Kimberly specializes in working with children living in therapeutic foster homes or group-home settings who are experiencing a variety of emotional and behavioral difficulties. She provides individual play therapy, co-facilitates groups for children and teens, as well as individual assessments. She has completed the Canadian Association for Child and Play Therapy (C.A.C.P.T.) Certificate Program.

Paparazzi
Source: Donicka Budd

Theme: Self-Esteem
Recommended Age Range: Ten to Eighteen
Treatment Modality: Individual, Group

Goals
- Identify personal strengths and challenges
- Identify personal values
- Create a personal story using pictures
- Explore the significance of people and objects in the client's life

Materials
- Disposable camera
- Scrapbook
- Pens
- Markers
- Stickers

Description
*This activity will require two sessions to complete.

Introduce the concept of "phototherapy" (using cameras to tell a story). Give the client a disposable camera and encourage her/him to take pictures of meaningful people, places, and other points of interest in her/his life. Like the celebrities in Hollywood where the paparazzi take pictures of them, their homes, families, where they shop, eat and so forth, the client will act as her/his own paparazzi by taking pictures of the many different aspects that make up her/his life.

Encourage the client to include the following themes: strengths, support people, hobbies, home, school, etc. Remind the client that as the "paparazzi," she/he is to capture all elements of her/his life. Develop the film before the next session.

At the next session, give the client a scrapbook to put the photos in, along with stickers, stencils, rubber stamps and other decorative supplies to enhance the scrapbook. The client will create a "tabloid magazine" using the scrapbook to hold the photos. The photos are to have captions or short descriptions to describe what they are about. Encourage the client to leave the first page blank as this will serve as the cover page. After all of the pictures have been pasted in and the captions created, encourage the client to look through the pages and then create a cover and a title for the scrapbook that captures the essence of her/his life.

Encourage the client to reflect upon the themes that are represented in the photographs. Ask how her/his strengths and challenges are revealed in the photos, or what values are represented. What does the client notice is missing (if anything)? What seems to influence a large part of her/his life?

Discussion

A client who presents with social and emotional challenges may lack insight and understanding about the impact people and events have on her/his life. This activity helps the client to portray his/her world through visual, concrete images, and enables her/him to share thoughts while associating meaning to events and people in her/his life.

About The Author

Donicka Budd, CYW, is a certified Child and Youth Worker with ten years of experience working with vulnerable children, youth, and families. Donicka works as a Family Support Counselor in a children's mental health agency and has led several workshops in the Toronto area. Her innovative, playful style is illustrative of her work with her clients. She is the author of *Empowering Adolescents to Realize Their Potential: Innovative Activities to Engage the "I Don't Know, I Don't Care" Responsive Youth through Expressive Arts and Play* and creator of her own line of therapeutic games. She currently serves on the Board of Directors of the Canadian Association for Child and Play Therapy.

Self-Esteem Crown
Source: Jodi Smith

Theme: Self-Esteem
Recommended Age Range: Five to Adult
Treatment Modality: Individual

Goals
- Increase positive thoughts about self
- Celebrate the client's strengths and abilities
- Create a concrete reminder of the client's strengths

Materials
- Paper crown (available from the Oriental Trading Company)
- Plastic jewels (available from the Oriental Trading Company)
- Glue
- Decorative supplies such as markers, glitter, stickers

Description
The practitioner provides the client with the crown and explains the concept of positive self-talk and positive affirmations. The practitioner tells the client that he/she will receive a jewel to add to her/his crown for each "jewel" (strength or positive trait) the client can identify about him/herself. The practitioner may begin by asking something as simple as "What makes you special?" or "What do you like about yourself?"

The practitioner may need to help the client begin to identify and verbalize strengths and abilities. The practitioner should help the client verbalize a positive self-statement by asking the client to identify the following traits:

- Identify something you are good at
- Identify one positive physical attribute
- Identify one positive personality trait

As the client identifies a strength or positive characteristic, have him/her write it on the inside of the crown (or the practitioner can write it), then have the client select a plastic jewel to represent this statement and glue it onto the outside of the crown. The more positive statements that are identified, the more jewels the client will have on the crown.

Once the client has finished gluing the jewels on the crown, allow him/her to further embellish it with glitter glue and stickers.

When finished, have the client wear the crown while reviewing the activity and while engaging her/him in answering these questions:

(1) Was it difficult to identify your strengths and positive attributes?
(2) What makes it difficult?
(3) How did it feel to say good things about yourself (positive affirmations)?
(4) How do you feel wearing the crown?
(5) What will you think when you look at it later?

Discussion

This activity can be used to assess a client's self-esteem and her/his ability to identify strengths or to enhance self-esteem. Although most clients will benefit from this exercise, for many clients this activity can be very difficult. For clients who struggle with recognizing any self-worth, the practitioner may lead them through various categories and assist them in identifying positive attributes, or work with them to reframe negative thoughts. If a client gets stuck, it can be helpful to ask her/him what others (friends, teachers, parents) would identify as strengths and positive attributes. Children with extremely low self-esteem will need more prompting and assistance from the practitioner. If the client agrees with what someone else would say, have her/him own it and add it to her/his crown. With younger clients or with clients who struggle with this activity, the practitioner can help them to identify skills they have mastered such as "I can tie my shoes" or "I can skip rope."

This activity can be very difficult for some clients. It may be important to discuss and differentiate the meanings of self-affirmations, self-esteem, and bragging/boasting. Sometimes children are encouraged not to say good things about themselves. It is important to spend time talking about each statement with the client and helping the client make it a specific and true reflection of her/his strengths and personality.

About The Author

Jodi Smith, MSW, LCSW, RPT-S, is a Licensed Clinical Social Worker and Registered Play Therapist Supervisor specializing in using play therapy in clinical practice with children, adolescents and their families, as well as with adults. Jodi is currently the Director of Norton-Fisher Child & Family Programs for West End Family Counseling. Additionally, she maintains a private practice in Claremont, California, and is a part-time lecturer for the USC School of Social Work.

I Am A Superstar!
Source: Susan T. Howson

Theme: Self-Esteem
Recommended Age Range: Six to Fourteen
Treatment Modality: Individual, Group

Goals
- Encourage focus on positive attributes
- Increase values vocabulary
- Increase awareness of positive attributes
- Recognize that self-worth is inside, not outside, of oneself

Materials
- Wooden/cardboard/foam photo frames (1 per child)
- Decorating supplies such as glitter, markers, glue, shapes, stickers
- Affirmative words written on paper, such as caring, friendly, energetic

Advance Preparation
Cut out affirmation words for children to glue onto their frames.

Description
The practitioner explains to the children that they are going to make a photo frame of how they want to feel, what they want to be more like, what they value, and which words describe themselves the most.

The children decorate their photo frames with the available materials and glue affirmations around the frame. The children place a photo of themselves into the frames so they are able to connect the positive attributes to themselves. The practitioner can ask questions such as "What are your favorite words?", "Which words do you want to feel more?" and "Which words describe who you are?"

Process questions can focus on which words were chosen. For example, "I know you are responsible because...."

Discussion
This activity empowers children to make use of the healing powers of positive self-affirmations. Self-affirmations can help children build the social and emotional resources they need to cope with the issues they are dealing with. Affirmations also help with the internalization of pro-social attitudes and values children need to achieve goals and solve problems. It is a reminder of their worth and of their ability to achieve in a difficult world.

<u>About The Author</u>

Susan T. Howson, MA, CPCC, CHBC, teaches at Ryerson University in Toronto. She has an MA in Instruction and Special Education, is a Certified Professional Coactive Coach, and is a Certified Human Behavior Consultant. Susan is also a Family and Relationship Systems Coach, an author, a keynote speaker, and a humanitarian-award winner. She has also won the International Coaches Federation PRISM award for the development of the Kids Coaching Connection Program and was a finalist for Canadian Coach of the Year. Susan has developed products (Manifest Your Magnificence Creations) that teach positive values and self-esteem.

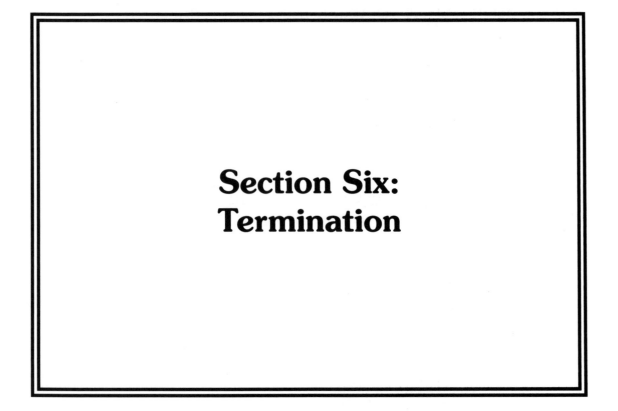

Section Six:
Termination

How I Felt the First Day
Source: Susan Kelsey

Theme: Termination
Recommended Age Range: Six and Up
Treatment Modality: Individual, Group

Goals
* Review therapeutic gains
* Discuss the mixed feelings that usually accompany termination

Materials
* Markers, colored pencils, or pens
* Paper (folded in half)

Description
Introduce the activity as follows:

"Today is your last day of therapy. On the top of the first side of your paper, please write 'How I felt the first day I came here.' Now, using words, symbols, or pictures, show how you felt the very first day you came to therapy."

When the client is finished, say, "Now on the other side of the paper, please write, 'How I feel today.' On this side, once again use words, symbols, or pictures to show how you feel today."

Discussion
This activity helps the client to see the therapeutic gains of treatment, as well as addresses the mixed feelings when treatment is finished. One client who did this activity on his last day simply put a big question mark in the first panel and a big happy face in the second. A picture can be worth a thousand words!

About The Author
Susan Kelsey, MS, MFT, RPT-S, is a licensed Marriage and Family Therapist and Registered Play Therapist Supervisor in private practice in Orange County, California. Her practice is limited to children from birth to 18 for nearly all issues related to childhood. Susan is an international speaker and presenter o n various topics related to the treatment of children and adolescents. She is currently President of the Orange County Chapter of the California Association of Marriage and Family Therapists and is founder and past president of the Orange County Chapter of the California Association for Play Therapy.

What I Learned Layered Gift
Source: Liana Lowenstein

Theme: Termination
Recommended Age Range: Seven and Up
Treatment Modality: Individual, Group

Goals
- Review therapeutic gains
- Provide a positive termination experience

Materials
- Gift for the client
- Wrapping paper (two different colors)

Advance Preparation
Select a small gift appropriate to the client, for example, a stuffed animal, or journal and pen. The gift can also be a graduation certificate, or the child's scrapbook containing work completed during sessions. Wrap the gift in five layers of wrapping paper. Alternate colors so the client can differentiate between the layers of wrapping paper.

Description
Give the wrapped gift to the client and explain the activity as follows:

"This activity will help you review your thoughts and feelings about therapy. Answer the questions below. For each question you answer, you get to unwrap a layer of the gift. Answer all the questions to get to the gift!"

1) You did many different activities in therapy. Which activities helped you the most?

2) Tell about a time in one of your therapy sessions when you felt proud of yourself.

3) Children have different feelings about ending therapy. Some children feel happy to end therapy, some children feel upset about ending therapy. How do you feel about ending therapy?

4) Tell about a positive change you have made since coming to therapy.

5) You have learned many ways to help yourself through tough times. What are some ways you can help yourself feel better when you are upset in the future?

Discussion

This activity is appropriate for the termination phase of therapy. It helps clients review and evaluate their experiences in therapy. The activity also helps to reinforce achievements made in therapy. As the child gets closer and closer to the gift, the intensity builds, and excitement mounts.

Reference

Lowenstein, L. (2006). *Creative interventions for bereaved children*. Toronto, ON: Champion Press.

About The Author

Liana Lowenstein, MSW, RSW, CPT-S, is a social worker and Certified Play Therapy Supervisor in Toronto. She maintains a private practice, provides clinical supervision and consultation to mental health professionals, and lectures internationally on child and play therapy. She has authored numerous publications, including the books *Paper Dolls and Paper Airplanes: Therapeutic Exercises for Sexually Traumatized Children, Creative Interventions for Troubled Children and Youth, More Creative Interventions for Troubled Children and Youth, Creative Interventions for Bereaved Children, and Creative Interventions for Children of Divorce.*

Termination Party
Source: Norma Leben

Theme: Termination
Recommended Age Range: Three and Up
Treatment Modality: Individual, Group

Goals
- Validate that the therapeutic relationship is built on trust
- Honor the client's (or group's) progress in therapy
- Provide a proper closure and positive termination experience

Materials
- Alphabet letter blocks
- Healthy snacks and beverage
- Personalized gift(s)
- Soft background music

Advance Preparation
Obtain permission from the client's caregiver to provide party food and check if the client has any food allergies. If preparing for a group party, obtain permission from each of the caregivers, finding out at the same time about allergies.

Description
The practitioner explains that this is the last therapy session with the client (or the last meeting with the group) and that a goodbye party has been prepared in her/his honor. The practitioner then explains the game as follows:

"We're going to play the Block Tower game. I have 26 alphabet blocks here and we're going to build a tall tower with them. We'll take turns, each time one of us will add a block to the top of the tower. With each block we'll say one thing (value, skill, principle) we have learned from all our past sessions. I'll put down the first block as the base. This block represents honesty as the base of our relationship."

The practitioner helps the child (or children) take her/his turns and recall social skills, good habits, or values learned. For example, the child has learned to be punctual, have fun, be respectful, have self-control, etc. The practitioner validates each of the child's contributions. As the block tower gets taller and taller, this game becomes very exciting and captivating. When the tower falls, the practitioner should say, "It's OK if the tower falls. As long as you remember what each of the blocks stand for, you can always rebuild it."

When this game is over, the "party" begins and should include the following four steps:

Step 1: The practitioner offers refreshments to the client (or the group) as a way to establish a nurturing moment.

Step 2: The practitioner summarizes their therapeutic journey, including these elements:

- The duration and the reason for therapy
- Initial feelings about the client or the group
- Accomplishments the client or group has made on this journey
- Current feelings toward the client or the group

The following is an example: "Chris, you started coming to see me nine months ago because your mom and school counselor were worried about your angry outbursts, at times even hurting yourself and others. You also seemed to be spending a lot of time by yourself, looking sad and lonesome. At that time, I shared their concerns, but I was also curious about what could have caused a young boy of ten to be so angry. Then I met you and found that you were using anger as a screen as a way to prevent anyone from getting to know you. After a few sessions, I discovered that behind that angry screen there was a Chris full of fairness, smarts, and curiosity. We've done a lot of work on expressing feelings, communication, and social skills. You just soaked up these skills like a sponge, turned around and used them at school and at home. I'm so proud and happy to learn that you did not have any meltdowns for four weeks. Now all your grades are As and Bs, and on top of that you've even made friends at school and in the neighborhood. Congratulations to you and to your mom."

Step 3: The practitioner asks the client (or the group) to share areas that she/ he believes have changed for the better, and, to share how she/he felt about the practitioner when they first met and how she/he feels about the practitioner now. (Note: In a group setting, each member will have a turn.) The practitioner will model accepting feedback from others – making eye contact, nodding, saying "Thanks."

Step 4: The practitioner presents a farewell gift to the client (or the group). This personalized gift will include a business card or an agency card with guidelines for future contacts. It is hoped that this will ease the pain of separation and prevent the client (or group) to feel that she/he is being abandoned. This ceremony ends after the client (or group) examines her/his gift, finishes the refreshments, and shares hugs or handshakes, depending on his/her level of comfort.

Discussion
Termination is an important step in the therapeutic process. If handled

appropriately, the client feels the relationship has been properly "wrapped up" in contrast to the unfinished business of past relationships. All children and adults have felt the hurt of abrupt departures of childhood friends and relatives. They had no control over those incidents. Nobody likes to feel hurt, so often we avoid that pain by not saying goodbye or not making new friends again. This ceremony will provide a model that teaches a healthy way of saying goodbye and give the client (or group) skills that will add confidence to her/his interpersonal relationships.

Reference
Leben, Norma Y. (1999). *Directive group play therapy: 60 structured games for the treatment of ADHD, low self-esteem, and traumatized children.* Pflugerville, TX. Morning Glory Treatment Center for Children.

About the Author
Norma Leben, MSW, LCSW, ACSW, RPT-S, CPT-P. Since graduating with a University of Chicago MSSA, she has worked as a CPS supervisor, school dropout team leader, residential treatment supervisor, executive director, and international trainer. She is a licensed clinical social worker and play therapy supervisor who has authored over 45 audio or video recordings, books, and publications in English and Chinese on parenting and play therapy techniques.

FREE BONUS GIFT

As a purchaser of **Assessment and Treatment Activities for Children, Adolescents, and Families** you're entitled to a special bonus from Liana Lowenstein.

Now you can get the eBook, **Favorite Therapeutic Activities for Children, Youth, and Families: Practitioners Share Their Most Effective Interventions**. This is a creative collection of assessment and treatment techniques for individual, group, and family therapy.

To download the eBook, go here now:

www.lianalowenstein.com

On the home page, you will see where to click to get the free eBook

You can also sign up to receive my **free monthly online newsletter**. Every newsletter contains fresh and relevant content including new articles, featured counseling techniques, discounts on mental health resources, and more.

Sign-up for the newsletter at: www. lianalowenstein.com

Enjoy your free resources!

Champion Press Books
Toronto